Advance Praise for
THE ONE MINUTE ENTREPRENEUR

"I promise you will be a better person for absorbing the wisdom of this book. By the time you have read *The One Minute Entrepreneur,* you will know this wisdom was meant for you."

— **Don M. Green, executive director, Napoleon Hill Foundation**

"*The One Minute Entrepreneur* is must reading for anyone who wants to improve their leadership skills. Great leaders are blessed by good followers, and this can only be accomplished by helping other people grow. This practical book will help in all aspects of your personal and professional life as an entrepreneur."

— **Ron Glosser, president, Hershey Trust (retired)**

"*The One Minute Entrepreneur* is filled with gems of wisdom. Read it if you're serious about reinventing your life."

— **Mark Sanborn, president, Sanborn and Associates, and author of *The Fred Factor***

"There is much said about stewardship in life and business; most of the time it's a reflection on money and material assets. However, the greatest stewardship is of influence. *The One Minute Entrepreneur* will teach you the importance of influence and inspire you to choose mentors wisely."

— **Jim Amos, chairman emeritus, UPS Store**

"We each have a lot more to learn and a lot more to teach. *The One Minute Entrepreneur* will help you do both."

— **R. Brad Martin, chairman of the board, Saks Incorporated**

"This book may be small in appearance, but it is big on ideas and ways to take advantage of other people's wisdom. It is a quick read, but the ideas will stay with you for a lifetime."

— **Paul J. Meyer, founder of Success Motivation Institute and *New York Times* bestselling author**

"Don Hutson and Ken Blanchard have captured the essence of an entrepreneur's influence. Many great entrepreneurs have impacted my life. It has been my honor and pleasure to pass this on. What a joy and blessing it is to see others benefit and grow from an idea or experience you pick up along the way."

— **Howard Putnam, former CEO, Southwest Airlines, speaker, and author of *The Winds of Turbulence***

"*The One Minute Entrepreneur* is an enjoyable read that provides a unique learning experience. Don Hutson and Ken Blanchard have done a beautiful job of teaching the concept of entrepreneurship and at the same time honoring the contributions of one of the heroes of the professional speaking field."

— **Zig Ziglar, author and motivational teacher**

Reinvent Your Life for Fun and Profit

Reinvent Your Life for Fun and Profit

The One Minute Entrepreneur™

Ken Blanchard
Don Hutson
with
Ethan Willis

The One Minute Entrepreneur

Published by
Executive Books
206 West Allen Street
Mechanicsburg, PA 17055
717-766-9499   800-233-2665
Fax: 717-766-6565
www.ExecutiveBooks.com

Paperback
ISBN-13: 978-1-933715-30-8
ISBN-10: 1-933715-30-8

Hardcover
ISBN-13: 978-1-933715-43-8
ISBN-10: 1-933715-43-X

Printed in the United States of America

Cover design by Douglas W. Clement

Interior layout by Gregory A. Dixon

Contents

Dedication

This book is dedicated to the thousands of entrepreneurs who have braved countless obstacles and hung in through good times and bad to create successful companies. These firms are the backbone of the free enterprise system.

We also dedicate this book to two such pioneers in particular: Charles "Tremendous" Jones and Sheldon Bowles.

Charles "Tremendous" Jones has been a mentor to both of us for years. From the quality, one-on-one time he has given to thousands to his extraordinary speeches to millions, we have seen him impact the world—ours included—one life at a time. His love of books—resulting in the founding of his own entrepreneurial venture, Executive Books, some four decades ago—has touched people around the world. His personal works, coupled with his encouragement of reading, have helped countless people improve their lives and achieve their dreams. His unbridled passion for business has inspired many entrepreneurs in their quest to build great companies. This mountain of a man stands so tall in his spiritual walk that it is impossible not to be inspired by his faith. His enthusiasm is boundless, his friendships deep, and his leadership profound.

Sheldon Bowles has had a tremendous impact on the thinking and business life of Ken and Margie Blanchard. He is an entrepreneur extraordinaire, *New*

York Times and *Business Week* best-selling author, and noted speaker. He began his career as a newspaper reporter covering stories in the Canadian Arctic, Japan, the United States, and Europe for such diverse media as the *Toronto Globe and Mail*, the Canadian Broadcasting Corporation, *Time,* the *Times* (London), and the *Winnipeg Free Press*. He left reporting to gain business experience and join Royal Canadian Securities, Ltd., where he rose to become a director and vice president. For fifteen years Sheldon was CEO of Domo Gasoline Corporation Ltd., which he built—along with Senator Douglas Everett, chairman—into one of Canada's largest independent gasoline retailers, with many hundreds of employees. At a time when the industry was going almost exclusively self-serve, they built their business and reputation on full-serve "Jump to the Pump"® service. It was his experience creating legendary service at Domo Gas that brought Sheldon to write, with Ken Blanchard, the best-selling book *Raving Fans*.

After leaving Domo, Sheldon—with three partners—turned a small manufacturing plant, Precision Metalcraft Inc., into a multimillion-dollar business. This success experience led him to coauthor with Ken his second bestseller, *Gung Ho!* Sheldon and Ken realized that you can't create raving fan customers without having motivated, committed, gung-ho people.

Sheldon's writing success led him to develop a third career as a stimulating speaker with great take-home value. His desire to help other entrepreneurs led Sheldon to coauthor two other books with Ken, *Big Bucks* and

High Five! There is nothing Sheldon enjoys more than mentoring other young business leaders, especially his son Kingsley, daughter Patti, and his honorary adopted son, Aaron. Patti and husband Kristjan have created a large commercial recycling company, Phoenix Recycling, and a successful Canadian document storage and high-security document destruction business, while Kingsley manages the family holding company and Aaron rebuilds jet engines.

We thank you, Charlie and Sheldon, for your unending positive influence, which has made our world a better place. May all the good you've done for others come back to you both a thousand times over. We know your influence through *The One Minute Entrepreneur* will make a real difference.

Foreword

There's something about essentials that we all seem to ignore. When it comes to entrepreneurship, we get consumed by our vision and forget about the money. We get consumed with our customer and forget about our employees. We get consumed about life and forget about death. Isn't it strange how you and I can become so disconnected from the essentials? That's why I love this little book. It's a wonderful story about the essentials of entrepreneurship.

After years of studying entrepreneurship, I'm sure about one thing: becoming a success story is easier said than done. Within any given year, close to 1 million people start a small business in the United States. Sadly, at least 40 percent of those businesses fail within the first year. Eighty percent of them will be out of business within five years, and 96 percent will have closed their doors before their tenth birthday.

One of the primary reasons small businesses fail is that they are started by technicians—people who are skilled at something and who enjoy doing that thing. Whether they are electricians, writers, photographers, or computer programmers, these people make the fatal mistake of continuing to do the work they're skilled at while ignoring other vital parts of the business.

The One Minute Entrepreneur will help you avoid that fatal mistake. In a parable as delightful as it is instructive, Blanchard and Hutson focus on three essentials you must attend to if you want to be a successful entrepreneur.

The first key is your finances. Many entrepreneurs go out of business because they don't know how to manage their money. Expenses exceed their sales, they don't collect their bills, and they don't realize that their success depends on cash, cash, cash.

The second key to entrepreneurial success involves your people. Empowering others to take responsibility in your business relieves you, the entrepreneur, of having to do everything yourself. Once your people feel empowered, they become like owners and are eager to take special care of customers.

Which brings us to Blanchard and Hutson's third vital element of entrepreneurial success: taking care of your customers. You can be the most skilled technician in the world, but if you don't take care of your customers, you're never going to make it.

The One Minute Entrepreneur will help you understand that while success might be easier said than done, focusing on a few essentials will dramatically increase your probability of success—and help you have fun doing it.

Michael Gerber
entrepreneur and author of *The E-Myth* and
*The E-Myth Revisited: Why Most Small Businesses Fail
and What to Do about It*

A Note to Readers

The One Minute Entrepreneur focuses on twenty key attributes common to successful entrepreneurs. These winning characteristics are set in bold type throughout the book and listed in the appendix. For a free, comprehensive online assessment of your entrepreneur attributes go to **www.estrengths.com**. This free assessment will help you discover your entrepreneurial strengths and unlock your full potential. It's our gift to you for purchasing this book.

Building a Firm Foundation

From the time he was a kid, Jud McCarley dreamed of becoming a successful entrepreneur. Yet he nearly blew his opportunity before he even graduated high school.

Jud was a good kid but an unremarkable student. In everything that counted most to him he was having a great senior year. He was popular, played tight end on a winning football team, and had a pretty girlfriend who thought the world revolved around him. That great year, however, was about to be interrupted.

On what started as a typical Saturday night, Jud took his girlfriend home from their date and drove to the Gridiron Grill to meet the boys. Tiring of the small talk, some of them decided to drive out to the gravel pit where they could drink a couple of beers.

Jerry "Race" Nelson invited Jud to ride with him. Race wasn't a close friend, but Jud had a major love of cars, and Jerry's new high-performance Mustang was incentive enough.

Jerry was charging down Holmes Road doing seventy-five in a forty-five-mile-per-hour zone, living up to his nickname, when he saw blue lights flashing. He pulled over, got out his license and registration, and looked sheepish as the officer approached the car.

"Get out of the car, son," the officer said.

Jerry obeyed. Jud sat still, wondering if he was supposed to get out or not. After giving Jerry a lecture and a speeding ticket, the officer leaned into the car to look at Jud.

"What about you? You always go along with what your buddies do?" the officer asked.

"Uh, I, uh?" Jud began, but before he could form a complete sentence, the officer turned his attention to a small vinyl bag sticking out from under the driver's seat.

"What's that?" the officer asked.

Jud turned to look. Before he could make sense of the situation, he heard Jerry say, "Marijuana." The word hung in the air.

Wait! Did Jerry just say "marijuana"? Jud's ears pounded with the beating of his heart. How could this be happening? He'd never done drugs! What would his parents say? What would everybody think if he had to go to jail? How was he going to talk his way out of this?

On the long, quiet drive to the police station, Jud and Jerry were both imagining all kinds of outcomes. Once there, the process was cut-and-dried. Jud realized that nobody was going to talk their way out of anything that night. They made their one phone call, were put in a cell, and began discussing how they could get out of there.

The kid in the next cell overheard them and said, "This ain't TV jail, boys. When you come here you spend the night, no matter who you are or what you did or didn't do!" He sounded like a veteran of this environment. Jud sank further into his bunk.

Jud's father showed up early the next morning. After a stern lecture from his dad, Jud was feeling like a criminal.

"Dad," Jud said, "you raised me right, and you deserve better than being down here with me right now. I swear I didn't do drugs. I didn't even know Jerry smoked marijuana. I'm really sorry this happened. Just get me out of here, and I promise I'll make it up to you."

Reginald McCarley, a sternly principled man, had a strong sense of right versus wrong.

"Jud, I believe you. But I'm going to tell you something that I never want you to forget. Are you listening?"

"Yes, sir," Jud said.

His father looked him in the eyes. "When I was about your age, my uncle taught me that at any given time, we are becoming the average of the five people with whom we are most closely associated. Don't ever underestimate the importance of whom you choose to be with."

It was a pivotal moment for Jud. Although he didn't realize it at the time, it would be the first of many meaningful one minute insights he would learn over his lifetime. Eventually, Jud would learn that the wise people like his dad who shared wisdom and experience with him could be trusted mentors. He knew guys who either didn't live with their dads or had dads who didn't particularly care. The incident taught him how lucky he was to have a loving, caring parent. It also led him to understand that if he associated with principled and successful people, he couldn't help but improve himself.

* * *

After football practice Monday afternoon, Coach Knapp asked Jud to come into his office. Jud had an idea what the visit would be about, and he approached Coach Knapp's office with trepidation.

"Close the door and have a seat," the coach said.

Without a word, Jud lowered himself into a chair.

"I hear you had a rough weekend," the coach said, "and I want to say a few things I hope you'll remember. One of the hardest decisions I ever had to make was whether to take this coaching job or stay with a company I'd been with for eight years. I gave up what could have been a good career there, but I felt I could make more of a difference as a coach.

"Jud, you're popular, you're a decent student, and you're a pretty good football player. But every teacher you have is convinced you could do better. When are you going to make something of yourself, instead of jerking around drinking beer at that gravel pit?"

Jud felt like he'd been kicked in the stomach. He swallowed hard.

Coach Knapp continued, "You want to enjoy a successful life, right?"

"Yes, sir," Jud said.

"Then make this a turning point. You're a nice kid from a fine family, and we enjoy doing business with your dad's company. You found out this weekend that you're not bulletproof, son. Now, I want to show you something."

The coach opened a drawer and pulled out a worn, blue linen book.

"My mother gave me this when I went away to college. She told me to take a minute every now and then to write down the important things that happened, and to put a star by the major lessons I learned, so that I could share them with her when I went home. I resisted at first but before long I got into it, not only to keep the promise to my mother, but to keep quotes I liked, things I learned, and thoughts about important decisions I made. This habit has changed my life."

The coach pulled out a clean, new notebook and handed it to Jud.

"Try it. If you decide to make something of yourself, this can chronicle the best ideas you hear along life's way."

Jud respected the coach and was moved that he'd taken the time to have this talk with him. He left Knapp's stadium office that day knowing his life would never be the same. He decided that, from that moment on, he'd be open to the counsel he got from others.

Before he turned out his lights that night, he pulled out his new notebook and took a minute to write down the advice he'd gotten that week from his dad and his coach. He called them his One Minute Insights.

The following weekend, Jud joined the family for Sunday dinner with his grandparents. The family hadn't told his grandfather about Jud's "incident," but they had given his grandmother a heads-up. Since she'd been a schoolteacher and a personnel director, nothing surprised her and few things got by her. While the others were visiting in the living room, Jud's grandmother took him into the kitchen for a chat.

"You're going off to college soon, Jud," she said,

"and you'll be exposed to many people and ideas. You'll encounter crossroads—points where you'll need to make choices. Try your best to make good, well-thought-out decisions. Often the decisions you make when you are young are more important than those made later in life, because they have more years in front of them."

"I'll do my best," said Jud.

"Also, make sure your values are strong and solid, because they'll be the foundation your life is built upon." She paused, letting the advice sink in. "When you have an opportunity to learn from someone who is exceptionally smart or successful, capture the gems they send your way."

She continued, "Jud, your *integrity* is one of the most important things you will ever have. Don't ever squander an opportunity to do the right thing. Remember that what's right is more important than who is right. If you want a life of success and *balance*, your values and integrity will be the vehicle to get you there. And remember: you never need to cheat to win."

Her special caring and perspective as a grandmother made her an appealing mentor—even more so than a parent—to Jud. That night he headed straight for his notebook and took another minute to capture the gems his grandmother had sent his way. Her profound suggestions would mold his character for years to come.

One Minute Insights

☞ Associate with people you admire and can learn from.

☞ Be open-minded about and receptive to counsel from others.

☞ Keep a notebook of the wisdom you read, hear, and learn.

☞ A good life is built on strong, solid values.

☞ What is right is more important than who is right.

☞ You never need to cheat to win.

Growing in Knowledge

Over the next few years, Jud studied hard and was near the top of his senior class at the University of Memphis, while holding down a part-time sales position at a clothing store. He was focused on graduation and making the right decision about his career. Lots of his friends had already accepted positions with major companies, but Jud wasn't 100 percent sure what to do next. He did know that he liked sales, but he still dreamed of making it big and owning his own company. He took pride in the fact that as an independent contractor selling at the clothing store, he made two or three times the money others did in their part-time jobs.

Dr. Avery Tonning, Jud's sales and marketing professor, had arranged for Jud and some of the other sales majors to periodically attend dinner meetings of the Sales & Marketing Executives of Memphis, where they had the opportunity to hear some excellent speakers. When Dr. Tonning encouraged Jud to write down key ideas from the speeches, Jud smiled. He already had three books full of key thoughts, and he eagerly added speakers' ideas at every opportunity.

Dr. Tonning had appeared in Jud's life at the perfect time. Not only was he Jud's professor, he was his academic mentor as well. The professor had developed a mutual admiration with Dirk Gardner, president of the National Sales Forum. Knowing Jud's passion for sales, Dr. Tonning encouraged him to attend a seminar that

Dirk Gardner's company was staging locally.

When Jud arrived at the seminar, his expectations were pretty low. Most of the sales speakers he had heard in school were marginal presenters. But the moment Gardner burst onstage Jud knew this was something altogether different. Within minutes, the audience was mesmerized. Jud had never seen or heard anything like this man before. As Gardner hammered home points about *self-motivation*, success in selling, and the virtues of the free enterprise system, Jud felt chills go up his spine. He was more fired up than he had ever been in his entire life.

The seminar featured four noted speakers: Dr. Kenneth McFarland, Bill Gove, Charles "Tremendous" Jones, and Zig Ziglar. Jud had never heard of them, but he figured if Gardner was the front man and these guys were supposed to be even better, they would be worth sticking around for.

The first featured speaker, Charlie "Tremendous" Jones, exuded a genuine enthusiasm. His favorite word was—you guessed it—"tremendous." He used it so frequently that when people started calling him "Tremendous" years ago, it caught on.

Jones told his rapt audience, "Five years from now you will be the same as you are today except for the people you meet and the books you read." He thundered, "If you're serious about success, you should develop a library of self-help books and works of literary giants! Once you decide you admire the content, the values, and the style of a writer, devour every one of that author's works."

Jud loved to read, so this was right up his alley. He

made a note to see what he could find in the university library.

Next up: Zig Ziglar. *Where do these guys get their names?* Jud wondered. With a dynamic delivery and homespun southern humor, Ziglar taught Jud, "You can get everything you want in life if you help enough other people get what they want." This struck a chord with Jud. He believed there were vast opportunities in selling when you were selling something you believed in.

At the dinner break Jud went to the lobby and patiently waited in line among sales professionals from all walks of life to buy one of Tremendous Jones's books. The great man autographed it, and they spent a few minutes talking. Jud felt totally connected with his sincerity and warmth. He took Jones's card and asked if he could contact Jones later. To Jud's surprise, Jones said yes.

The third speaker was Bill Gove, the first president of the National Speakers Association. He was a sales expert, but with his ability to make the crowd laugh, he could have been a comedian. Talking about his humble beginnings, he said, "We were a big family in a small house. I never got to sleep alone until I got married!" The audience howled.

Gove offered his wisdom: "Everyone loves to buy, but they hate to be sold. Lead with your ears! Ask questions, assess needs, develop relationships. If you're really good at it, people will practically beat your door down to buy from you."

What a refreshing departure from the hard closes and high-pressure tactics Jud had heard about. Gove argued that selling could be a great and honorable profession for those who did it right. In reality, everyone had to sell. Everybody attempts to sell their ideas every time they open their mouth, so why not get good at it?

The wrap-up speaker was Dr. Kenneth McFarland, known as "the dean of American speakers." McFarland inspired Jud with his hopeful vision of the American free enterprise system. At one point McFarland looked over the podium, seemingly right at Jud. He motioned with his index finger and softly said, "Come here and let me tell you something." Jud was almost out of his seat when he realized that the entire audience was leaning forward. This speaker was captivating!

McFarland said, "If you can sell and sell well, nobody can ever quarterback you out of a great future. Success can only occur when opportunity and preparation meet. Remember that, and you'll enjoy a life of high achievement."

Jud ignored the ache of writer's cramp as he took copious notes. He knew these anecdotes would be fuel for future success. Without question, this day was a life changer. His curiosity had turned into a passionate desire to fully develop his own gifts.

McFarland ended to a thunderous standing ovation. As the audience began to disperse, Jud went in direct pursuit of the seminar producer, Dirk Gardner.

His heart pumped hard as he approached the man. Why beat around the bush?

"Mr. Gardner," he said, "I'm Jud McCarley from Dr. Tonning's sales class. I graduate with a sales major from the University of Memphis in six weeks, and I want to go to work for you. This seminar was the greatest experience I've ever had, and I can help you sell others on attending your events."

Gardner said, "Well, Jud, I'm delighted you're impressed with what we do. Let's you and I have breakfast in the morning." Jud could hardly control his excitement as they booked it on the spot.

Jud left the auditorium feeling like he was walking twenty feet off the ground. He had the strong sense that today had been a stepping-stone to his destiny.

* * *

Jud arrived ten minutes early for the breakfast appointment and requested a quiet table. Within moments, Dirk Gardner approached, flashing a wide smile.

"You're early," he said as he took his seat. "You're off to a good start."

Over coffee and omelets, Jud answered Gardner's questions about his background, skills, and beliefs. The more they talked, the more deeply Gardner probed.

"How do you deal with rejection and failure, Jud?" he asked.

"I like to *focus* on success, of course, but I guess I deal with rejection okay," said Jud.

"We all grow strongest in the crucible of adversity," said Gardner. "The single biggest *salesmanship* lesson you must learn is that periodic rejection is very much a part of the success process."

"How so?" Jud asked.

"No matter how good you are, you'll experience a lot of failure. The greatest sales professionals are those who experience a 'no' and immediately go on to their next call with total confidence, giving as good a presentation as they ever have, unfazed by the previous rejection. Sales champions know that success is not determined by how much verbiage you can dish out. It's all about how much rejection you are willing and able to eat! You must go through the nos to earn the right to experience the yeses."

"I've never thought about rejection like that, but I'm eager to put your advice into practice," said Jud.

Gardner asked, "Are you willing to travel into cities you've never been to, where you don't know a soul, and start selling with enthusiasm?"

"Yes, I am," Jud replied.

For the first time, Jud felt a tinge of nervousness. He thought of his boss at the clothing store, who had preached, "It's not what you know, but who you know that counts."

Jud asked Gardner what he thought of that concept.

"That cliché has been around for a long time," Gardner replied. "Who you know can be important, but what matters is who knows you and what they think of you—your confidence, your professionalism, and your belief in what you are selling."

Jud scribbled more notes. He realized that learning was cumulative. Things he'd learned in the past were being superseded by better information from a more knowledgeable source. He smiled as he finished his notes. Dirk Gardner was definitely sending him gems.

Gardner motioned for the waiter to bring more coffee.

"I'm glad you're excited about our seminar business and that you benefited from the event yesterday," he said, "but you also need to be grounded in reality. You can't imagine how challenging it is to put all those people in those seats.

"When you're presenting the program to people," Gardner continued, "they're evaluating our offering by the job you do that day, not by the job our speakers will do later. They can only imagine what that day will be like; they don't have a clue of the actual power of the upcoming event. Your responsibility is not to sell it short. The only way they can benefit from our seminar is to be there, and that sales task is up to you. You must arouse curiosity in them along with a desire to be in attendance. Still interested?"

"Yes, sir," Jud said.

"Are you motivatable?"

"You bet!" Jud answered.

"Trainable?"

"Absolutely!"

"Jud, does this sound like the type of career you want to pursue?"

Jud smiled. "If that's an offer, the answer is yes!"

"If you'll do what I tell you to do, I'm convinced that you will succeed. I'm willing to mentor you on the sales process if you promise me you'll work hard and follow my direction."

On a deep level, Jud knew this was going to be more than a job; it was his destiny unfolding. He would be an independent contractor on commission. He knew that drill. He would seize the opportunity!

One Minute Insights

☞ To develop your skills and nourish your soul, read great books.

☞ Success occurs when opportunity and preparation meet.

☞ It's not who you know that counts; it's who knows you and what they think of you.

☞ When you feel moments impacting your destiny, seize the opportunity.

Learning the Craft

Jud's new job in promoting the workshops consisted of a two-stage selling process. First, he called on a sales organization, talked to the manager, and attempted to set up a half-hour presentation at the manager's upcoming sales meeting. Jud would give a sample talk—a prelude to the high-powered seminar they were bringing to town—and give his listeners an opportunity to make a reservation. He made a commission on the number of seminar enrollments he sold.

Dirk Gardner was no fool. He hired his new salespeople on a straight commission basis, so he had very little downside. He was confident enough in his selection process that he felt he could pick winners, and since his salespeople had to get good or go hungry, he was ensured of having a highly motivated *team*. He was committed to giving them everything they needed to succeed.

In his first two weeks, Jud made loads of calls, but for some reason, they weren't translating into many sales. Despite his enthusiasm, this new career wasn't taking off as he'd expected. He was learning a new type of humility.

No good mentor lets a new subject fail, so Dirk Gardner began an intense one-on-one coaching process with Jud.

"Jud," he said, "the humility you mentioned is not a bad thing, but a good thing. It is with humility that we admit we don't have all the answers. It's humility that gives us the desire for a higher degree of focus, and it's with that intense focus that we learn and grow."

"How, exactly, do I focus?" asked Jud.

"Remember that for every yes you get, you will probably have to endure eight to ten nos. Know your numbers and conversion rates. If you take care of your numbers, your numbers will take care of you. As one of my favorite business gurus, Dr. Peter Drucker, said, 'If you can measure it, you can manage it.'"

"Thanks," said Jud. "That gives me something solid to go on—know my numbers."

It would be one of the finest lessons Jud would learn. He kept up with his numbers with a vengeance. At any given time he knew exactly what his conversion rate of prospects to buyers was. He remembered fondly his father's advice about seizing opportunities to learn from people you admire. Dirk Gardner was just such a person. With Gardner's input, Jud worked diligently to improve the content and delivery of his sales presentation, because he was convinced that those two items, along with call count, would determine his success.

* * *

After four months of steady work, Jud hadn't made much money. He'd originally thought that to be successful in selling you just had to be cheerful, nice, and helpful. He was now learning how it worked in the big leagues.

He continued to plug away with enthusiasm and focus and began to show some progress. But by year-end he still wasn't making more money than most of his college buddies. It was hard work, and there seemed to always be some financial pressure. He found that making the transition from naïve student to productive sales professional wasn't all that easy.

The next big seminar was a month away. Jud pulled out the business card from Charlie Tremendous Jones and dialed his number, wondering if the popular speaker would even remember him, let alone make time for a meal together before the seminar.

"Of course I remember you, young man!" Tremendous boomed over the phone. "I'm pleased you followed up. That's half the battle—suiting up and showing up."

A week later they were shaking hands at a restaurant. Knowing how busy Tremendous was, Jud deeply appreciated every moment he could share with him. So the second they sat down, Jud started to talk business.

"Hey, slow down!" said Tremendous. "We'll have time to talk business later. Tell me about you."

Jud filled in Tremendous on his life, hopes, and dreams. After a time he became nervous, afraid they'd run out of time without covering his agenda. Once again, Jud brought up the subject of his career.

Tremendous replied, "Jud, you're in the enviable position of simultaneously getting sales experience and speaking experience. You will learn a lot in this business. The sky is the limit as to where you can go."

Jones's words stirred hope in Jud. As a newcomer to the business world he'd believed the sky was the limit, but in the last few months that dream had been fading. A streak of recent rejections had shaken his confidence. Faith, hope, and optimism were being crowded out by fear, pessimism, and self-doubt.

Jud mustered the courage to ask the bold question he had been thinking about for weeks. "Charlie, would you consent to being a mentor to me? If you do, I won't let you down. Dirk is my mentor on selling skills, but I'd love to have your input on a broader perspective. I really want to grow as a person, and you're already one of my role models."

Tremendous smiled broadly. "You've passed the first test. Mentors tend not to show up unless you ask them to. And since I'm already in the loop, I guess we should formalize the arrangement!"

"Thanks," said Jud. "I appreciate your generosity."

"It's called 'giving back,'" said Tremendous. "I wouldn't be where I am today without my mentors. I'll be one of your mentors, Jud, but there's something you should know: I take life in small bites. We won't spend a lot of time together, but I can pack a lot of information into just a minute."

"Funny you should say that," Jud responded with a smile. "My old coach taught me to take a minute every now and then to write down what's important. I have a notebook full now. I call them my One Minute Insights."

"That's tremendous!" Jones boomed. "Then we're off to a good start. Now you have to promise me that I'm not tackling this project alone. I learned a long time ago that to be an effective mentor, you must first have an enthusiastic protégé. You already know where I stand about the importance of reading. It's the books you read and the people you meet that impact you the most. I want your commitment that you'll become a voracious reader. That doesn't necessarily mean you'll read a great number of books, but it does mean you'll read deeply for understanding. I have several literary mentors, and you should, too. You've got to agree to read every week. Is that a deal?"

"You bet," Jud said. He loved books, so this was an easy deal to make.

"I also want you to agree to spend time sharing with others the things I share with you. Helping others is just as important as being helped," said Tremendous. "Are you in?"

"I'm in," said Jud.

"Good," said Tremendous. "You'll get more out of my mentoring by making and honoring commitments like these."

After talking for a few more minutes about Jud's challenges in selling seminar enrollments, Tremendous wrapped up their discussion with one last piece of wisdom.

"Psych yourself up before every meeting with client groups. Be your best every time. You're on stage, so act like it! When you put energy and conviction into your presentation, your overall message will constantly improve. Great salespeople give every effort their best shot!"

Jud thought about all the rejections he'd been dealing with lately. "How do you get psyched up?" he asked.

"Great question," replied Tremendous. "When I was selling full-time, I would imagine making the sale—seeing my clients wearing big smiles as we shook hands after signing the deal. Now that I'm mainly a speaker, I do a similar thing. I imagine the audience leaping to their feet for a standing ovation at the end of my speech and clapping enthusiastically.

"There's been a lot of research on Olympic athletes," Tremendous continued. "The ones who tend to win are the ones who—before the race—see themselves sailing across the finish line, winning the race."

"What a great concept," said Jud. He smiled, realizing that Tremendous was indeed going to be a tremendous mentor.

One Minute Insights

☞ Humility helps you focus and be open to learning and growing.

☞ Take care of your numbers, and your numbers will take care of you.

☞ For a mentor to be effective, you have to be an enthusiastic and committed protégé.

☞ Always visualize your desired outcome ahead of time.

Catching the Entrepreneurial Bug

After three years at the National Sales Forum, Jud was like a racehorse kicking at its stall door. He wanted to get out on the track and run. He had learned his job well and was making a decent living, but falling far short of his sky's-the-limit dreams. Yet Jud was **ambitious**. He needed and wanted to do more. He felt driven to start his own company, but feared that he'd fail. He liked his boss and appreciated what Dirk had done for him, but he could see that working for him indefinitely would only hold him back. He knew that tens of thousands of entrepreneurs before him—including Dirk—had faced these same doubts and forged ahead, but Jud wasn't sure he was that much of a **risk taker**.

So he decided to call Tremendous to ask for his advice.

"Your being self-employed is inevitable," said Tremendous. "The big question is, what kind of business are you going to develop? I read a powerful book by Sheldon Bowles, a great entrepreneur, called *Big Bucks*. It was all about making serious money for yourself and your organization. I learned four key things from Sheldon. The first two are relevant to this question. When you want to start a business, you have to **play to your passion**. This is what Sheldon called the test of joy. What do you like to do most? If you try to be an entrepreneur just to make money and not to satisfy the fire in your belly, you will fail. Sheldon feels that if you don't love what you're doing, you will never put in the necessary time to be the best.

"Jud," continued Tremendous, "what have you been doing for National Sales Forum that you really love?"

"I've been selling and speaking," Jud replied. "I think my speaking ability has been my best sales asset, and that's what I love to do the most. When I get face-to-face with a customer to present our program, I can usually close a sale. I think I'm a good **communicator**. I've had the opportunity to give some speeches outside my work, which is great. I do a talk called 'So You Want to Sell Something?' It's a great overview of all the things I've learned about selling from Dirk and my work at the National Sales Forum. It's not just about sales. It includes a lot about positive motivation—including **self-motivation**—and people really love it."

"How do you feel when you're on your feet in front of a group?"

"Energized! I have to be careful, because I lose track of time, I love it so much. I want to start my own speaking business, crazy as that might sound."

"I don't think you're crazy, Jud. I think you're onto something. That's why I became a speaker. I'd rather sell myself than someone else or some product."

That's all Jud needed to hear. "Judson McCarley and Associates. How does that sound?" he asked excitedly.

Tremendous laughed. "That's great, Jud. Now let me give you another piece of advice. Don't resign your sales job with Dirk until you have some outside speaking success under your belt. This gets to the second thing I learned from Sheldon. You need to find people who will *pay for your passion*. This is what Sheldon called the test of purpose. At some point, making money has to be more important than having fun. That's when you have to ask the question: Will anybody give you money to do what you love? It might take you a little time to develop a couple of inspiring speeches that people will want to pay to listen and learn from. If nobody will pay you to speak, you have a hobby, not a business. I sing at the top of my lungs in the shower, but Gloria and I would be on Skid Row if I tried to make a living as a singer."

"What do you suggest I do next?" said Jud.

"First, join Toastmasters. I'm sure there's a chapter where you live. They meet over breakfast and give everybody a chance to make a short speeches and get feedback. They're a wonderful group, and you'll learn a lot.

"Second, see if you can get some time off the second week of next month, because I'll take you as my guest to the National Speakers Association convention. They love people who want to get into their business. You'll be able to network with some wonderful speakers from around the country."

"Done!" said Jud.

One Minute Insights

☞ Ambition can result in life-changing events.

☞ Identify what you love to do most and do more of it.

☞ Don't quit your day job until you've got some success under your belt.

☞ If nobody will pay you to do what you love, you have a hobby, not a career.

Gaining a Vital Teammate

The following month, Jud caught a flight to Orlando to join Charlie Tremendous Jones at the annual meeting of the National Speakers Association. When he arrived at the convention hall, the room buzzed with energy. Jud felt his pulse quicken as he recognized some of the famous authors and speakers he'd admired for years: Denis Waitley, Brian Tracy, Stephen Covey, Harvey Mackay, and Patrick Lencioni.

He scanned the meeting rooms and finally spotted Tremendous chatting with an attractive young woman in a smart-looking suit.

"Jud," said Tremendous with a big grin, "I'd like you to meet one of the rising stars in our business, Terri Aviotti."

"Hi," Terri said, extending a hand. "Good to meet you, Jud." Terri's sharp blue eyes seemed to look right through Jud, and her smile melted his heart.

"The pleasure is mine," said Jud, shaking her hand. He felt an immediate attraction to Terri and had to remind himself that his focus for now was embarking on his new speaking business. He was certainly not in the market for a relationship at this time. His business was the love of his life. A romantic involvement would just get in his way. All his attention was directed toward building his skills and his business, and that's the way he intended to keep it.

Yet of all the important contacts he made at the

convention, the one who really captured Jud's attention was Terri. It wasn't just her pretty blue eyes. Jud thought Terri might make a terrific speaker for Dirk Gardner's seminar company. As he spent more time with her he realized that she was one of the smartest and most dynamic people he'd ever met, as beautiful on the inside as she was on the outside. On the last day of the convention they exchanged business cards.

Two weeks later they met to discuss business over lunch in Terri's hometown, Atlanta. Jud discovered that he and Terri admired many of the same role models and shared many of the same values. Their working lunch and afternoon meeting advanced through dinner. As Jud left Terri at the end of the day, he was racking his brain to think of how he could see her again. He kept trying to put her out of his mind, but he could never do it for long, and he found himself thinking about the next time they'd meet.

The two began to see each other as regularly as their busy schedules would allow. Over time Jud came to realize that whether he'd planned it or not, he now had a second love in his life. It eventually became difficult to justify commuting to Atlanta every week to support their relationship. Each time he and Terri talked on the phone, Jud hated to hang up.

One day Tremendous called and put Jud on the spot.

"When are you going to get serious about that wonderful woman I introduced to you?" he asked.

"I adore Terri," Jud said, "but marriage is a pretty big step. How do I know I'm making the right choice?"

"I'll give you a piece of advice I learned at age fifteen from my uncle," said Tremendous. "I'll never forget that day. We were out on the lake, fishing for bass. My uncle told me that it's okay to fall in love with looks and personality, but to marry character. He told me to go for a 'long-term horse,' not a short-termer. If the character isn't there, move on. Does that help clarify things?"

"Yes," said Jud, "it does. Terri's got it all—*especially* the character. She's a long-termer."

In the end, love overcame Jud's fears. That Christmas Jud proposed to Terri in the home of Charlie Tremendous and Gloria Jones, while they were gathered around the piano singing Christmas carols with close friends. Six months later they were married and living in their own place in Jud's hometown, Memphis.

* * *

Jud had always imagined that when he broke through the glass ceiling into his life as a successful entrepreneur, he'd do it alone. Terri, too, had planned to continue developing her speaking businesses on her own. But that all changed when, shortly after they said "I do," good friends suggested they go to a workshop for couples called Marriage Encounter®. This was an intensive weekend where spouses learned a wonderful way to communicate.

While the strategy Jud and Terri learned was helpful, what impacted them the most was a discussion about "married singles." These were people who ate meals together and slept together but led two separate lives, and never the twain did meet. The Marriage Encounter facilitators suggested that healthy couples spend at least 30 percent of their waking hours doing things together. They argued, "Why be on different PTA committees? Why have one coach Little League sports without the other? When you do things together, you get to bask in each other's strengths and your relationship becomes richer."

That advice hit home with Jud and Terri. They decided that rather than developing separate careers, one day they would build a speaking business together. They would be a ***team***.

One Minute Insights

☞ Few people, if any, come into your life without a reason.

☞ When it comes to finding a life partner, character trumps personality and looks.

☞ If you want a great marriage, make sure you commit to spending time together outside of meals and sleeping.

☞ Be a team. If you think you can work together, give it a try.

A Door Opens

While building a world-famous, lucrative speaking business together was Jud and Terri's new dream, the reality of their early business life fell far short of that vision. Neither one of them was satisfied with their financial situation. Terri's income was in a holding pattern. Jud was making decent money now, but he had the nagging feeling his speaking gifts were not being utilized to their fullest potential. They longed to break through to serious success; they just needed a break.

A door opened one fall when Jud and Terri were invited to participate in a weeklong university in San Francisco for the Young Presidents' Organization, also known as YPO. An organizer for the event, Red O'Rourke, had heard Jud speak at a National Speakers Association meeting. He'd been so impressed with Jud's youthful charisma that he invited him to speak at the YPO event in San Francisco. Jud was in between seminars at the National Sales Forum, so he was able to take a weeklong vacation.

Jud had an inkling this might be the opportunity he'd been praying for. He was to be one of forty faculty members who would be speaking to approximately six hundred YPOers and their spouses. The faculty resources included Wayne Dyer, Jim Collins, Jim Rohn, Tom Peters, and other luminaries. Jud could hardly believe it. He'd love to get their autographs, let alone be on the faculty with them. When Jud told Red O'Rourke that his wife also was a speaker, Red asked to see some video footage of her on the platform. After seeing Terri in action, Red immediately asked her to do a special session on balance—her specialty—as part of their lifestyle track.

The first day of the university, Jud was ready. He poured all his years of preparation into his well-honed motivational speech "So You Want to Sell Something?" and about two hundred of the twelve hundred attendees showed up. YPOers and their spouses could choose between three or four sessions every class period. When Jud finished his session, he got the standing ovation he had visualized. The audience loved it and went racing out of the room buzzing with enthusiasm about the dynamic new speaker. Jud was stunned by the positive response.

"Why not?" said Terri as she hugged him. "Look at all the early breakfast meetings of Toastmasters you attended, and all the coaching you got there, plus the support your new National Speakers Association buddies have given you. Not to mention the hundreds of presentations you've given to small groups promoting the seminars."

"I guess you're right, Hon. I did put a lot of hours into creating three or four exciting speeches."

"You sure did," said Terri with a smile. "Charlie Tremendous would be proud of you."

On the second day, Terri did her session entitled "Strategies for Balancing Complicated Lives" and also received rave notices from the presidents and spouses who attended.

"Way to go!" cheered Jud as he high-fived Terri and gave her a hug. "I've got the right partner in more ways than one."

The third day, Jud gave a talk on **leadership**. This time about eight hundred people showed up. On Friday—the final day of the university—Jud did a session on strategies for managing change, and essentially the whole convention came. Hardly anyone went anywhere else.

At the end of the university, Red O'Rourke said, "Well, Jud, you won."

"Won what?" asked Jud.

Red said, "You were the most popular speaker, and Terri hit a home run, too. What are you two going to do now?"

Jud said, "I'm going back to my job at the National Sales Forum with Dirk Gardner, and Terri will continue to do freelance speaking."

Red said, "You're crazy. When you're hot, you're hot! I've been talking to some of the YPOers here. We think you two should start your own speaking and training company. What do you say?"

Jud smiled and shook his head. "That's our dream. We do hope to have our own speaking business someday, but right now Terri and I can barely stay on top of our schedules and balance our own checkbook. How are we going to run a company?"

"Don't throw away your dream," said Red. "I bet some of my YPO buddies from around the country would love to help you get started. What's so great about this organization is that everyone loves the free enterprise system, and they get excited when they find folks who have the ***determination*** and guts to step out on their own. Say the word, and help will be available.”

When Jud told Terri about his conversation with Red, they both felt torn.

“I don’t know, Terri,” Jud said. “This could be our moment of destiny—or it could be our moment of doom! I’m just afraid that if we dive in and fail, we’ll prove all the naysayers right.”

Terri nodded. “We’re definitely at a crossroads,” she said.

Jud suddenly remembered the day in his grandmother’s kitchen years ago, when she told him how important it was to think through such decisions with care. He knew that they were being given a choice, and that the decision they made about this would affect their life for years to come. If ever he needed his mentor, it was now.

That evening Jud called Charlie Tremendous.

“What’s up, Jud?” Tremendous asked.

“Terri and I are here at a YPO university in San Francisco. Apparently our performances here were spectacular enough that a group of influential businesspeople is encouraging us to start our own speaking and training business right now.”

“So you both were hits?” Tremendous asked.

“I gave three speeches and the crowds increased every time. For my final talk, I essentially drew the whole convention. Terri gave her specialty speech on balance and wowed them.”

"So folks really liked you both?"

"To hear these people talk, we're the best thing since sliced bread. They want to help Terri and me draw up plans for our own company, and they've promised to get us plenty of speaking opportunities over the next year or so. What do we do, Charlie?"

"I'm excited for you, Jud," said Charlie, "but if you really want to start your own business, you need to know what it takes to be a successful entrepreneur. I recommend that you call a friend of mine, Harris Palmer. He's an entrepreneur from Australia who's forgotten more than most people know about starting a business. I bet he'll give you some great advice. He certainly helped me."

* * *

The next morning Jud dialed the number Charlie Tremendous had given him for Harris Palmer. He was amazed when he got right through.

"If you're a friend of Tremendous, you can't be all bad. How can I help you?" said Harris in his thick Australian brogue.

"I want to start my own business, and Tremendous says you can do that in your sleep. Do you have any pointers for me?"

"This is going to be a short conversation," said Harris, "because there are only four things I want you to remember to be a successful entrepreneur.

"First, your **sales have to exceed expenses**. A lot of people, when they start a business, want to get fancy stationery and business cards and a nice office, and they don't have any customers. That's a formula for disaster.

"Second, *collect your bills*. There are all kinds of people who go out of business and other people owe them money. Be reasonable, but don't be your customers' banker.

"Third, *take care of your customers*. They pay your bills and write your checks. Remember: you work for them.

"Fourth, *take care of your people*. I'm amazed at the number of entrepreneurs who abuse their people and then expect them to take care of their customers. As you build your business, your people are not your company's most important asset. They *are* your company. When you shut the doors at the end of the day and your people head home, your business goes with them."

Jud was frantically scribbling notes as Harris talked.

"Wow," he said. "Tremendous was right about you. What helpful advice on starting a business. Thanks!"

* * *

Shortly after the conversation with Harris, Jud and Terri tentatively moved ahead with their dream and began to formulate a plan for their new company, JTA— which stood for Judson, Terri & Associates. Given what they had learned at Marriage Encounter, they both thought that the name of the organization should include Terri's name as well as Jud's. Learning from Jud's conversation with Harris, they would keep it simple—no fancy business cards or stationery, or even an office.

After they had enough money coming in, all of that would take care of itself.

They were both energized and scared. They debated the pros and cons for hours on end. On the plus side, they'd be fulfilling a dream they passionately shared. On the negative side, they'd be putting at risk what little financial security they had.

Fortunately, their *optimistic* attitudes overshadowed their fear. They called Charlie Tremendous on a speaker-phone to share Jud's conversation with Harris and their excitement about launching their new business.

"Harris was great," said Jud. "We think we now know what it will take to be successful as entrepreneurs. We've been back and forth about this next move, but we've finally decided we're ready to take the plunge!"

"We're totally committed now and there's no turning back," added Terri enthusiastically. "What do you think, Tremendous?"

There was a pause on the other end of the line. Then Tremendous shouted, "Rev up your engines—it's time to take off!"

One Minute Insights

☞ Think through significant life decisions with great care.

☞ You never achieve more than you think you can, so create a big dream.

☞ When opportunity knocks, go for it.

☞ Don't let your expenses outstrip your revenue.

☞ You can't afford to be a banker for your customers. Timely collection of invoices is crucial.

☞ Without your customers you're in trouble, because they pay the bills.

☞ Nurture your people. They make it all happen.

Launching the Company at Last

Jud dreaded turning in his resignation. As much as he'd longed to break free, Dirk had become like a father to Jud. After all, without Dirk's encouragement, Jud never would have found his passion. Feeling almost queasy, Jud stepped into Dirk's office and broke the news.

Any fear he had about Dirk's reaction was eliminated when his old boss leaped to his feet, ran around the desk, and gave Jud a hug.

"Tremendous told me this was inevitable, especially when you picked up such a vital teammate as Terri," Dirk said.

Then Dirk did the unimaginable. He returned to his desk, reached into a bottom drawer, pulled out his checkbook, and wrote Jud a check for ten thousand dollars. "Maybe you and Terri could put this to good use as you get started," he said with a smile. "I can't tell you how much I appreciate all you have done for me and the National Sales Forum."

Jud was speechless for several moments and felt his eyes welling with tears. "I'm so blessed to have a mentor and friend as wonderful as you," he finally managed as he returned Dirk's hug. "How can I say thank you?"

"The best thanks you can give me is to succeed and be two of the best speakers in the country," said Dirk.

"We are certainly going to give it the old college try," said Jud with a smile. "Any parting advice?"

"Never ask a person who's hooked on mentorship

for advice unless you want some," said Dirk with a twinkle in his eye. "Two thoughts: Watch your ego. If you get too many standing ovations and people hanging on your every word, you might start to believe your own press and act like you're a big deal. We once hired a speaker who was great on the platform but had such an enormous ego he was impossible to work with. We were considering him for twelve seminar appearances, but canceled him after the first one."

"So don't let your ego eat your brain," summarized Jud.

"Right," said Dirk. "Be competent, but also be a person of **humility**."

"What's your second piece of advice?" asked Jud.

"You may have given a similar speech many times before, but deliver it with the same passion and enthusiasm as if it were your first time," said Dirk. "What you're speaking about might be old to you, but it's probably not old to your audience. And if you touch just one person's life, it's probably the reason you're there."

Jud couldn't believe it. Not only was Dirk not mad, but he was generous beyond imagination and still willing to mentor him with good advice.

* * *

When Jud got home he was so excited to share with Terri what had happened with Dirk, he almost couldn't talk. That night they both signed the JTA incorporation papers.

When the ink dried, Jud reached over and held Terri's hand. "From the moment you walked into my life, you've helped make my dreams come true. This is what I've always wanted, Honey—my own company. I can't thank you enough. And to think we get to do it together."

"You're welcome." She squeezed his hand and dazzled him with her smile. "But give credit where credit is due. If you hadn't dreamed it, we wouldn't have achieved it."

With that, JTA was born.

* * *

Jud and Terri were amazed that, with Red O'Rourke's help, three other YPOers agreed to join Red as the advisory board to JTA. Each of them had a different strength area to bring to the party: Juan Escobar had a passion for financial matters; Lou Stafford, for customer service; and Nancy Kaline, for people development. Red would be the convener and go-to guy.

They all agreed to fly at their own expense to join Red, Jud, and Terri later that month at a resort near Jud and Terri's hometown of Memphis. The purpose of the meeting was to help them develop some clear business goals and strategies to accomplish them. Jud and Terri were asked to do some thinking about their goals and strategies before the meeting.

When Jud and Terri shared their initial goals for their business at the meeting a month later, their YPO friends laughed. There was no mention of profit! The two young entrepreneurs talked about working with people that they loved, making a difference in the world, and having fun.

"Who's going to pay for all this?" asked Juan with a laugh. "Making a profit is a necessity if you want to stay in business." He went on to tell Jud and Terri that this was not only important in the beginning when they first started their company, but would be important throughout the life span of the company.

"Juan is right," said Red. "While profit should not be your only focus, without good cash management, you are in trouble."

That weekend, not only did their YPO friends help them clarify their goals so they were real business goals, but they also helped them develop a budget, analyze staff needs, and formulate a marketing plan for getting more business.

When analyzing staff needs, the advisory board helped Jud and Terri take a good, honest look at their respective skills. They both were good speakers—everyone knew that. Their feeling was that Jud's strong point was the *visionary* or strategic part of leadership. He was able to dream big dreams. Terri's strengths, on the other hand, were in the operational aspect of leadership. She was a better organizer and manager of people. For those reasons, they recommended that Jud be the chairman of JTA, and Terri be president and chief operating officer. That's exactly what they did.

As everyone was leaving, Jud and Terri's advisory board made a commitment to help secure work for their new company. They even put a date on their calendar for the next YPO University that would be held in Melbourne, Australia, in the fall. Jud and Terri felt honored and blessed by their support.

* * *

In the beginning Jud and Terri ran JTA out of their house. It was a real mom-and-pop operation. They kept the office supplies in their hall cupboards and stored and mailed handouts for their speeches out of their garage. Kinko's was their only office.

As they had promised, their YPO friends and advisory board kept Jud and Terri busy. After about six months, they felt that JTA's cash flow was good enough to allow Jud and Terri to lease some office space, but it was certainly not spacious. They had just enough room for two small work areas. They hired an office manager/secretary, which left a cramped space for Jud and Terri to share.

Jud and Terri thought often about the short but sweet advice Jud had received from Tremendous's Australian friend, Harris Palmer. They did everything they could to assure that *sales exceeded expenses*. Linda, their office manager/secretary, worked diligently to *collect their bills* and make sure they were paid for the work they did.

While Jud and Terri occasionally were scheduled to speak on the same programs, like YPO events, they most often headed off in different directions. Sometimes it seemed like they were ships passing in the night. A couple of decisions changed that.

First, Jud and Terri realized that if the only way they could make money was for their bodies to show up all the time, their bodies would eventually wear out. So they came up with an *innovative* new vision: they wanted to make money while they slept. They imagined what it would be like if checks were working their way through the mail system while they were resting. So they decided to expand their business, and called up Tremendous for ideas.

"Slowly expanding your business is a great idea," said Tremendous. "When it comes to making money, there's a third thing Sheldon Bowles taught me. You have to *plus your passion*. He called that the test of creativity. How do you create new avenues of revenue that build on your passion? Always remember that your income is a function of revenue minus expenses. Unfortunately, when it comes to increasing their income, most people focus all their attention on cutting costs."

"Isn't it important to manage your costs?" Terri asked.

"Absolutely," said Tremendous. "But while managing costs is important, it can be a negative energy drain."

"That's for sure," said Jud.

"To counter that," Tremendous continued, "you need to be *resourceful* and *purposeful*, putting positive energy into creating those new avenues of revenue that build off what you already are passionate about and good at doing."

That's exactly what Jud and Terri decided to do. They partnered with some other speakers to book speaking engagements when Jud or Terri either couldn't make the event or weren't a perfect fit for it. For their efforts, they would get 25 percent of the fee. They essentially became a small speakers bureau.

Jud and Terri also decided to develop some learning materials—assessment instruments, audios, and videos—that would enhance their programs and that they could sell to clients and other speakers.

These new strategies required additional staff, which they slowly began to add. They certainly didn't want to have expenses exceed revenues.

The new businesses and resources also needed supervision, and that was hard when Jud and Terri were both gone from the office. But that all changed when Terri became pregnant with their first child.

Morning sickness initially limited Terri's travel schedule, and then the arrival of Alex put a real halt to her budding speaking career. Except for local speaking opportunities, both Jud and Terri decided that it didn't make sense to have Terri away from home. That decision made even more sense when five months later Terri was blessed to become pregnant again and nine months later Alex's little sister, Elizabeth, was born. Now Terri stayed home to manage the company while the on-the-road, heavy lifting for the business fell completely on Jud's shoulders.

One Minute Insights

☞ It's good to have a *strategist* or two in your life.

☞ Making a profit is a necessity if you want to stay in business.

☞ Use creativity to come up with new sources of revenue.

Growing Pains and Ego Issues

Over the next five years, the company slowly grew to fifteen employees and ten affiliate speakers. Over that period of time, they moved their offices twice. It wasn't always easy, and Jud's youthful dream of vast riches was still a long way off. During the first few years of the growth, Terri remained president. But it became obvious that her ability to juggle the main responsibility for the care of Alex and Elizabeth and overseeing the management of JTA became an overwhelming challenge.

"First things first," Jud and Terri told each other. "The kids are more important than the business," they agreed. So Terri decided to step down as president, and within a month JTA had a new president and chief operating officer, Forrest Oakes. Forrest had worked as a consultant with Jud and Terri in marketing their products and services, and had impressed them with his business acumen.

Linda—their first employee and still their operations manager—and several of their speaker affiliates had reservations about Forrest. They felt he was a good businessman, but that he just didn't share the strong values that Jud and Terri had built the company on: ethical behavior and honorable relationships. Rather than focusing first on doing things the right way and building respect and trust with their people, customers, suppliers, and community, Forrest's focus was mainly on their third-ranked value, success. He was purely a "bottom line" guy. Since Jud and Terri felt that business finance was not their greatest strength, they thought this emphasis was needed at JTA. As a result, they didn't listen to the concerns of any of their people and instead continued to support Forrest.

Even with the added expense of a new COO, the revenue brought in by the new businesses and the increase in Jud's fees seemed to cover it. But just covering his salary was not good enough for Forrest. His focus was clear—growth, growth, growth—and fate played into his hands.

Jud was addressing a thousand business owners at a conference in Dallas, and a *Wall Street Journal* writer was sitting in his audience. After listening to Jud's brilliantly honed talk on "So You Want to Sell Something?" the journalist tracked Jud down and interviewed him. She asked him how he'd become a professional speaker and grilled him about his business philosophies. Responding to her questions, Jud thought he was doing well—but with reporters, you never knew. He waited anxiously for the article's publication.

When the article hit the stands, hundreds of phone calls came pouring in. It was clear from the overwhelmingly positive response that Jud's comments had struck a nerve. Jud's high profile in the press translated directly into increased business for JTA. Forrest cheered when requests for company training and materials doubled, then quadrupled. When the orders grew beyond JTA's ability to fulfill them, rather than panicking Forrest charged on even harder.

Jud suddenly forgot Dirk's early career advice to stay humble. He became enamored with his own press and bought into Forrest's ego stroking. He started to take on a Superman persona. There was nothing Jud felt he couldn't do.

As a result, Jud was gone all the time. He found it difficult to turn down any invitation. He began to think every request for him to speak or conduct a training seminar was from someone who needed HIM, and Forrest reinforced Jud's belief that he was supremely important. He even demanded that clients pick up Jud in a limo.

While Jud was the main man, Forrest also creatively marketed their other speakers, as well as the learning materials JTA had developed. The company was really on its way to becoming a business far beyond Jud's original dream.

When Jud wasn't on the road, he was in the office long hours working side by side with Forrest to stimulate more business. It was only a matter of time before his ambitious president brought forth his most cherished business plan.

"Jud, you and JTA have become recognized leaders in the training and development business. We're getting several attractive suitors that want us to roll up with them and some other companies in the industry and go public. If we want to continue to grow, we need more capital. If we begin to prepare ourselves now, the sky is the limit. With the right partners and story, you and Terri will need a wheelbarrow to cart out all the money."

That image—plus the rush of adrenaline Jud felt when he thought of standing on the floor of the stock market on Wall Street the day their public offering was announced—drove Jud even more.

During the first years of their lives, Jud had been a model father for Alex and Elizabeth. He always seemed to have time to play with them, and he and Terri seemed like the perfect couple and parents. The fact that they balanced their seemingly wonderful family life with working together was an inspiration to others. But that all changed when the *Wall Street Journal* article hit the streets and Forrest began overfeeding Jud's ego. Now life was work, work, work for Jud.

While Jud in his heart still really loved Terri and the kids, he saw less and less of them. With Alex and Elizabeth both in school, it didn't take long for Jud to lose touch with their daily lives. A missed teacher meeting here, a soccer game there, even a birthday celebration sometimes went unattended. He repeatedly made promises to take family vacations, most of which he felt the need to break.

In a feeble attempt to spend more time with Terri, Jud made a pact to have one date night per week. The pact soon became a joke. They fell months behind on their date calendar. Jud's broken promises and months of missed dates caused Terri to give up believing his promises. The neon sign was hanging in his marital window, but Jud was oblivious to it.

It wasn't unusual for Jud to get most of his sleep on airplanes. In fact, during one especially grueling week of speaking engagements he spoke twice in Hawaii, with engagements in San Francisco, Denver, and Boston in between. That trip generated a lot of revenue, but left Jud exhausted. After coming home he slept for twenty straight hours. Terri checked on him several times to see if he was still breathing.

When Jud finally got up the next morning, Terri poured him a cup of coffee and begged him to slow down.

"This is our chance, Honey," he said. "We can have everything we ever wanted. We've just got to make hay while the sun shines."

"But Jud, I'm worried about you," Terri said. "You can't keep this up. And honestly, I'm tired of being a single parent. The kids hardly ever see you."

"I know, Sweetie, but now that our efforts are finally coming to fruition, I can't risk letting these opportunities slip through our fingers. Please be patient. Our time will come."

Terri not only was worried about Jud, she also was worried about JTA. Now that the kids were in school, she was looking forward to getting more involved with the company again. But the place had changed. She had her first clue when Linda, their longtime employee, quit. Disturbed, Terri called her to find out why. When Linda tried to explain, she started to cry.

"I'll write you a letter," Linda said. "I'm just too emotional right now to talk."

Terri waited anxiously for the letter to arrive. When it did, she sat and read it slowly:

Dear Terri,

I'm sorry I couldn't talk the other day, but I was an emotional wreck. I was part of yours and Jud's dream from the beginning, and I am so sad that it seems to be dying.

Forrest is a mad man running wild. All he can think of is sales, sales, sales and growth, growth, growth, and he doesn't care how he does it.

Forrest has taken the heart right out of your staff. He doesn't care about anyone—only the numbers. And the saddest thing is, he's got Jud behaving the same way, too. It's just not the same dream or the same values that we had when we started. I know change is inevitable, but I think Jud is heading for disaster with Forrest at the helm.

I know that this is hard for you to hear, Terri, but I love and respect you and am sad beyond my ability to express myself to you face-to-face.

Big hugs to Alex and Elizabeth. I hope you can win Jud back from Forrest.

Love to you,
Linda

When Terri confronted Jud with Linda's letter, he dismissed it.

"The company has just outgrown Linda," he claimed.

Terri couldn't believe that she seemed to be living now with a stranger. Jud had become a driven entrepreneur obsessed by achievement. Unfortunately, he had not yet learned the principle that any strength taken to an extreme could become a liability. He was seriously out of balance. Terri had tried to get him to reach out to Tremendous or Red or any of their original advisory board, but he kept avoiding them. Unbelievably, he didn't even answer Tremendous's phone calls.

Jud looked great on the outside, but his insides were roiling. The better the company did, the harder he worked. He considered every problem a personal challenge. With Forrest pushing him on, Jud became possessed.

One evening, he got home after nine o'clock. Terri was sitting alone in the kitchen.

He kissed her on the back of the neck and said, "Hi, baby, what's up?"

She sat still for a moment, and then turned in her chair to look at him.

"Jud, I just got back from Elizabeth's dance recital. By myself. That was right after I went to Alex's Boy Scout medal ceremony. By myself. Did you know that Alex twisted his ankle yesterday and can't play soccer this weekend? And that my sister had a suspicious mammogram this week? And oh, by the way, I'm sorry you couldn't make our anniversary dinner last night. I enjoyed it thoroughly—by myself!"

His eyes grew wide. "Wait a minute, Honey—"

"*You* wait," she said, her voice quavering. "I've

been waiting. And I'm tired of it. This is not the kind of life I planned. You need to make some serious choices soon, or someday you'll come home to an empty house." With that, Terri got up from the table, walked to the bedroom, and quietly closed the door.

Jud sat there, stunned. "Can this be happening?" he asked out loud.

Dirk's warning not to let your ego eat your brain came rushing back to him. Jud realized for the first time that he could win the battle—help the company go public—and lose the war—his family. It was hard to admit, but he suddenly realized that his life was completely out of balance. He was failing as a husband and father. With that realization came a blinding flash of the obvious: success is not just about having a great career. It's about having a great life.

When Jud crawled into bed that night, he gave Terri a hug and whispered into her ear, "I hear you loud and clear, Honey. I'll give Tremendous a call in the morning. I've gotten my priorities all goofed up."

"You sure have," said Tremendous, after Jud told him the whole story. "Any man spending ten to twelve hours a day at the office—not to mention so much time on the road away from home and neglecting all of his other commitments—is on the wrong track. You've got to get more balance in your life."

Tremendous paused for emphasis. "Jud, you've got racehorse blood in you, man, but you've got to get out of the mule mode! Remember, a hound dog in the heat of a hunt isn't worrying about how many fleas he has! Get busy with your charities, diversify your activities, pay attention to your health, spend more time with your wife and kids, and commit to the Sunday school class. Focus on what you have to be thankful for. Get some balance back in your life!"

"What would give me more balance?" asked Jud.

"Ruth Peale, Norman Vincent Peale's fabulous wife, wrote a great book years ago entitled *Staying in Love*," replied Tremendous. "She argued that you can have it all in life as a married couple if you keep your priorities in order. First comes God, then your spouse, then your kids, and finally your job."

"I once read an article about Tom Landry, the old Dallas Cowboys coach," interjected Jud, "and he had the same priorities. That's why he always seemed so calm when he was coaching. He said, 'If I lose on Sunday, I have a lot left over.'"

"Good point," said Tremendous. "Unfortunately, there are too many coaches who believe it's the end of the world when they lose on Sunday, because their work is all they think about. I am afraid you're heading that way, Jud."

"That has been my sad realization," admitted Jud. "How can I turn things around?"

"First, you need to get God back central to your life. Terri told me that after the kids were baptized, you became active in the church. You joined a men's support group and even started to help teach a third-grade Sunday school class. What's happened to all that?"

"It all went out the window, I'm embarrassed to

say," Jud replied. "I got too busy for God."

"Did your dad forgive you after you got into trouble with Race Nelson?"

"He sure did," said Jud, remembering his night in jail.

"Your heavenly father is the same way," said Tremendous with a smile in his voice. "He'd just like to be your first response rather than your last resort. I find it really helps if I take some time every day to tell him what I'm thankful for and share whatever's happening that day where I think I could use some help. When your ego gets in the way, you really **E**dge **G**od **O**ut."

"I hear you loud and clear," said Jud. "And then my relationship with Terri—do you have any thoughts about that?"

"Sure do," said Tremendous. "Go home and tell Terri you've been an out-of-balance jerk and ask for her forgiveness. Then both of you give me a call."

* * *

"I know that you two have really been through a lot lately," said Tremendous as Terri and Jud listened to him on the speakerphone, "and you're both very emotional. I don't have any silver bullets for you, but I do have some ideas for you to think about. Do you both love your kids?"

They said, "Of course we do, Charlie. You know that."

Tremendous knew he had their undivided attention. "Let me tell you something I learned from my spiritual mentor many years ago when Gloria and I were having our challenges. The greatest thing a mother can do for her kids is to love their father. The greatest thing a father can do for his kids is to love their mother. Love is not an emotion, it's a decision. Jud, do you want your relationship with Terri to work?"

"Of course I do," said Jud.

"How about you, Terri?" asked Tremendous.

"I've had my moments lately," said Terri. "But yes, I do. Jud, I still see you as my husband and friend."

"Okay, that's two yeses," said Tremendous. "Marriage counseling only works with two yeses. So get yourself someone good and commit to have a session once a week until you think you're back on track with your marriage."

For the first time, Tremendous's seriousness overshadowed his joviality.

Jud and Terri sat in total silence for several minutes. Slowly their hands came together as the wisdom of Charlie Tremendous Jones resonated with both of them. They agreed to get counseling and to begin working on their marriage with renewed energy and focus. The only thing Jud wanted to do more than hug his wife was to be with his kids and hug them again.

Jud admitted to Terri that he was out of balance and reluctantly confessed that he had to do something about the business and his and Forrest's obsession with growing JTA to go public. He agreed to call Red O'Rourke and ask for some help.

One Minute Insights

☞ Watch your ego. It can bite you when you least expect it.

☞ Relationships thrive through love but can deteriorate under stress when they aren't nourished.

☞ Keep your priorities in order: God, spouse, family, work.

☞ Work to balance your family life with your business life.

☞ Continually seek the wisdom of your mentors.

Turning Things Around

Jud felt relieved when he reached Red on his first call. "Before we get together," insisted Red, "you need to get an outside audit of JTA's books, so we know where you are with cash. I know Juan Escobar would want that done. We both have some uneasy feelings about Forrest Oakes."

Jud's relationship with Forrest became strained after he told him about the audit. Finances had never been Jud's strength or interest. He had turned that entire aspect of the business over to Forrest. Bringing in an outside group to look at the books was putting into question what Forrest had been doing in that area, and Forrest didn't like it one bit. Jud's relationship with Forrest hit a low point when the audit was completed and Red suggested that the report be presented at an open meeting attended by Jud, Forrest, Terri, Juan, and himself.

The numbers did not look good at all. While all the work Jud and Forrest had done to increase sales had worked on that front, it appeared that Forrest was spending money like a drunken sailor and expenses were out of hand. Not only were sales not exceeding expenses, but accounts receivable were out of whack, too. Some of JTA's biggest clients were over sixty days delinquent on bills, and on average, invoices were being paid at a forty-five-day level.

Looking directly at Jud and Terri, Red summarized the situation by saying, "You seem to have forgotten the first two things that Tremendous's friend, Harris Palmer, told you were required to be a successful entrepreneur: sales have to exceed expenses, and you have to collect your bills."

Then Juan, also focusing his attention on Jud and Terri, continued the straight talk. "I'm sure I told you both at our first advisory meeting—when you were just getting started—that making it in business requires three very important things."

The expressions on Jud and Terri's faces suggested that if Juan had told them, they had forgotten.

Juan said, "I want you to write these down—in capital letters."

Jud reached for his legal pad. "I'm ready," he said. "What are the three things?"

"*CASH, CASH, CASH*—that's what it takes to make it in business! A healthy profit has to be a team effort. While increasing revenues is important, everyone has to watch the margins by managing costs and collecting receivables, so you have some money left over at the end of the day. Jud, it doesn't matter how smart you think you are or how innovative your products are if you don't get paid in a timely manner. You must put forth a team effort to collect your receivables right away. Without good cash management, you'll never make it. You've got to solve this problem. Right now I think you've got about three months before your banks and other collection agents start calling."

"I agree, Juan," said Jud. "Forrest, we've got to get on this with all of our key people and see how we can improve our collection process immediately."

Forrest looked down and said nothing.

Juan immediately turned his attention toward Forrest. When Forrest looked up and gave him eye contact, Juan said, "If this were a public company and I was on your board of directors, I would ask for your resignation."

With that, Forrest lost it. He went into a tirade and started yelling at Jud and Terri. Then he stormed from the room.

When Forrest was gone, Terri reached over and grabbed Jud's hand.

"I think what you've seen and heard here today, combined with my letter from Linda, leaves us with only one choice, Jud," said Terri. "Forrest has to go, and we have to get back to basics."

That's exactly what they did. Red helped them develop a good severance package for Forrest, and Juan designed a short-term plan to stop the financial bleeding, including opening the books to everyone in the company.

At first Jud resisted opening the financials to everyone.

"I know what you're thinking," said Juan. "If you're like most managers, the last thing you want to do is share financial information with your people. But smart managers realize that large financial gains can be made by sharing what used to be considered sensitive data. They believe that when people understand the business realities of how their company makes money, they are much more apt to roll up their sleeves and help out. When this happens, everyone feels a sense of ownership, because they begin to realize how their efforts impact the company's bottom line.

"I'll give you an example," continued Juan. "Back in the days when I owned a restaurant, I was having a hard time convincing my general manager about the merits of sharing important financial data with employees. To unfreeze my manager's thinking, I went into the restaurant one night at closing time and asked everyone to join me in the dining room. I divided all the employees—cooks, dishwashers, waiters, waitresses, bus people—into groups of five or six around tables and asked them to come to an agreement about the answer to this question:

"'Of every sales dollar that comes in to this restaurant, how many cents do you think fall to the bottom line—money that can be returned to the investors as profit or reinvested into the business?'

"The least amount any group guessed was forty cents. Several groups guessed seventy cents. In a restaurant, the reality is that if you can keep five cents on the dollar you get excited. Ten cents, and you're ecstatic! Can you imagine the attitude among these employees toward such things as food costs, labor costs, and breakage if they thought our restaurant was a money machine?" asked Juan.

"I bet that changed some people's attitudes," said Jud.

"It did," Juan replied. "I was really pleased when one of the cooks said, 'You mean, if I burn a steak that costs us six dollars and we sell it for twenty, at a 5 percent profit margin we have to sell six steaks for no profit to make up for my mistake?' He had things figured out."

"I see your point," said Jud. "But opening the books is sort of counterintuitive for me. It just doesn't feel comfortable, especially when the numbers aren't all that great."

"That's because you're more concerned about looking successful than getting help to *be* successful. If you keep your people well informed and let them use their brains, you'll be amazed how much they'll help manage costs and brainstorm ways to increase revenues," said Juan.

Jud and Terri carried out Juan's suggestion the day they called an all-company meeting to announce the departure of Forrest. They were amazed at the positive energy that came flowing from their people when they realized he was gone. It was obvious that Linda had been right about Forrest. Not only had he been mismanaging the finances, but he also had been wreaking havoc with their people. The news that Forrest had left the company almost received a standing ovation.

After opening the books and sharing the balance sheet that had come out of the audit, Jud said to everyone, "Terri and I, in turning around this situation, don't want to get rid of people. We want to solve this together by forming several task forces to look into how we can continue to increase our sales and also several to study how we can cut our costs. It is clear to us that we need to reduce expenses seventy thousand to eighty thousand dollars a month over the next quarter to dig our way out of this financial mess."

Excited that Jud and Terri were back at the helm, people jumped in with both feet to help out. It was agreed that everyone would take a salary cut. Jud and Terri took a 15 percent cut in pay, and all the key managers took 10 percent cuts. All the frontline employees followed suit, with a minimum 5 percent cut. Everyone also agreed to a number of other cost-cutting measures. For example, if someone quit, they wouldn't replace that person. And during this turnaround period, JTA would not match contributions to the employees' 401(k) fund.

Seeing everyone's commitment to turn JTA around, Jud and Terri made a special announcement.

"When we right the ship and our finances are back in good shape, we want to take everyone to Hawaii to celebrate."

"You certainly couldn't do that if you were a public company," said Tremendous with a laugh when he heard about their plan. "Imagine explaining to your stockholders a celebration to Hawaii. Once you go public, it's hard to have that kind of freedom to do what you think might be best for your people—especially when it costs a fistful of money."

"I now realize that," said Jud.

"Going public is a smart move for some companies when they need additional capital to expand and build the business. But do I think it is appropriate for a personal services business like yours?"

"Do you?" asked Jud.

"Do you want my priceless advice, rather than my good advice?" asked Tremendous.

"Sure, I want your priceless advice," Jud said with a smile.

"Actually, I'm going to give you both. My good advice is, don't ever ask anyone for their advice. When you ask for their advice you're asking them to tell you what to do. You don't want a mandate. Now here's my priceless advice: Ask people for their counsel. That way you're gathering information so you can make your own well-informed decision."

"Okay, I want your counsel, Tremendous."

"Then I would recommend that you get this idea of going public out of your head. Get Terri back involved in the business and grow it gradually over time. JTA can give you everything you ever wanted from a business. Plus, it will give you the time to have a balanced life. When I talked to Rabbi Kushner, the author of *When Bad Things Happen to Good People*, he told me that during all his years as a rabbi, he never heard anyone on their deathbed say, 'I wish I had gone to the office more.' They all wished they had spent more time with people they loved."

"That really is priceless counsel," acknowledged Jud. "Any other good thoughts?"

"Yes," said Tremendous. "Try substituting strategic patience for crisis management. You're on the right track now. Just keep doing the right things, one day at a time.

"And," Tremendous added, "don't forget the last

two things that Harris Palmer told you to remember to be a successful entrepreneur: take care of your customers, and take care of your people. In fact I heard a wonderful quote recently that could pull together all the thinking you got from Harris, Red, and Juan. Write this one down, because it's a good one: Profit is the applause you get for taking care of your customers and creating a motivating environment for your people."

"That is a good one," said Jud.

"I think you're already making some good moves with your people, so why don't you contact Lou Stafford and get his advice about customer service? Then you can talk to Nancy Kaline about any thoughts she might have about creating a motivating environment for your people."

Jud and Terri thought Tremendous's counsel was truly priceless. They jointly agreed to drop the idea of being part of a public roll-up and committed to growing the company gradually over time. They realized that they not only needed to stay on top of their finances, but could use some priceless advice about serving their customers and restoring the faith and trust of their people. Besides keeping in touch with Red and Juan about finances, they planned to ask Lou and Nancy to help them with their customers and their people.

But before Jud and Terri had those conversations, they wanted to see if they could get Jeremy Britton to join them as their general manager. He was an old buddy of Jud's—they had played football together in high school—and Jeremy had been the best man at their wedding. Terri had always admired Jeremy, and trusted him. He was a **curious** person who was **adaptable** when it was appropriate. He had been a successful manager in both the hospitality and health-care fields, and Jud and Terri felt he would be a perfect match for their culture. They knew that Jeremy's tenacious attitude would set them on the right track, and that he was also an excellent **problem solver**.

Before Jeremy agreed to join Jud and Terri, he took some vacation time to come and interview all the employees and get a sense of the challenges that might lie ahead.

"As I'm sure you both know, we have two major problems," said Jeremy to Jud and Terri. "First, as Red told you, the company is bleeding cash. It sounds like you have some strategies started that could solve that problem."

"It's probably only a start," admitted Jud.

"But starting is good," said Jeremy with a smile. "Second, you don't have the systems set up to handle all the demands you're getting. In talking to your people, I'm getting a sense that you could blow a good thing. While your people are excited that you are taking back the leadership, they are getting burned out from working long hours. Plus, you're rushing to fulfill orders and making too many mistakes. There are too many instances of shipping the wrong materials to the wrong people. You're putting a lot of folks on hold for too long. Basically, you have to develop some strategies for serving your customers better and get your people the help and support they need to effectively implement those strategies."

"Sounds like we have some real challenges," said Jud.

"Are you up to the challenge of helping us?" asked Terri.

"I'm fascinated by your business and think you've got great people. I can't think of anyone I'd rather work with than you two," said Jeremy.

With that, Jud, Terri, and Jeremy had a group hug.

While Jeremy went to work on getting on top of their systems and finances, Jud and Terri decided the timing was right to talk with Lou and Nancy.

Terri realized firsthand the problems they were having and why they should talk to Lou first when she overheard one of JTA's staff members, Maria, taking care of a phone call in a manner so perfunctory it almost sounded cold.

"Crank caller?" Terri asked Maria with a smile.

"No, that was Bill Lakeman, one of our customers," Maria replied.

"It almost sounded like you were angry with him," said Terri. "Is there a problem?"

Maria's eyes widened. "Gosh, I'm sorry," she said. "I didn't realize that's how I sounded. It's just that I'm so swamped. I have at least a dozen phone calls to return, a stack of orders to process, and a few special projects to handle. I guess I don't feel like I have *time* to be nice."

Terri smiled sympathetically. "Take a deep breath, Maria, and don't worry about the backlog. This isn't an emergency room and nobody's going to die if a task doesn't get done. Can someone around here help you out?"

"Not really," Maria replied, shaking her head. "To be honest, we're all feeling a lot of pressure lately."

"Thanks for letting me know," said Terri. "We've asked Jeremy to see how we can take some of the pressure off you all so you can give our customers the best service possible."

"That's what we all really want to do," said Maria. "Thanks."

When Terri finished telling Jud about her experience with Maria, he sighed.

"Let's call Lou Stafford," Jud said. "We're lucky to have him on our advisory board, since he's been working in the customer service area for years."

They both sat down at a speakerphone and gave Lou a call.

One Minute Insights

☞ *CASH*, *CASH*, *CASH*—without good cash management, you'll never make it as an entrepreneur.

☞ Poor leadership can send you off in directions you don't want to go.

☞ Going public is not the right decision for every company.

☞ Profit is the applause you get for taking care of your customers and creating a motivating environment for your people.

☞ The right leader at the right time can help steer things in the right direction.

Creating Legendary Service

Lou Stafford was delighted that Jud and Terri had called. "Growing pains are a great problem to have," he said. "But taking care of your customers is not optional—it's imperative. Especially now as your company is growing, you've got to let your customers know that they are your number-one priority. Make them feel loved and respected. If you don't, pretty soon you won't have any customers. And without your customers, you don't have a company."

"But how do we do that when there's so much work piling up?" asked Terri.

"It's a question of focus," replied Lou. "You have to impress upon your people the importance of treating customers right. To keep your customers today, you can't be content to merely satisfy them; you have to give them legendary service and create 'raving fans.' These are customers who are so excited about the way you treat them that they want to tell stories about you. In essence, they become part of your sales force."

"What do you mean by 'legendary service'?" asked Jud.

"I'll give you an example," said Lou. "My mother, when she was ninety, went to her refrigerator one day to get some ice. When she opened the ice section, water came pouring out; something clearly was wrong. Since she was an independent cuss and wanted to solve the problem herself, she went to the Yellow Pages. She called appliance service companies one after the other, only to be told that the earliest anyone could visit her was in three weeks.

"Now if you are ninety years old, three weeks is a long time," Lou continued. "Discouraged, my mom was about to call me for help when she saw a little ad that said, 'Same day service.' She called the number and soon a friendly voice was saying, 'We'd be happy to fix your refrigerator today, Mrs. Stafford. When would you like us to come?'

"'I have a choice?' my mom responded in amazement.

"'Absolutely,' he said.

"'How about two o'clock?' Mom replied.

"Not only did a serviceman show up at two, he even had tools and knew what a refrigerator was. He fixed the fridge and as he was leaving, he handed his business card to my amazed and happy mom. It had his home phone number on the back. 'Anytime, night or day, you have a problem with your refrigerator, you can give me a call,' he said.

"What do you think my mother was doing for the next three days?" Lou asked. "She was calling everyone she knew who was still alive about the great service she had received. She had become a raving fan."

"But how did this company pull off that kind of amazing service?" Terri asked.

"I wondered the same thing when my mother told me this story," replied Lou. "So I called the owner to find out how he could service people the day they called. It turned out that he had been a fix-it man in Massachusetts. Because of his health, his doctors suggested he move to a warmer climate. When he got to San Diego, he would find out when people were moving into a house they had just bought. He would then knock on the door and tell them that he was a fix-it man. If they needed any painting or repairs done, he would be happy to do it at a reasonable price. All he asked was that they agree to refer him to other customers if they liked his work.

"This guy always showed up on time, did what he said he would do with high quality, and charged a reasonable price. People loved his work. He built his business up so much that when old customers would call to get him to do something, very often he didn't have time because he was so busy. A number of people suggested to him that he start his own company. But he was reluctant, because he was concerned about managing employees and having a big payroll."

"I can understand his reservations," said Jud with a laugh. "This entrepreneur business requires a lot of people management and *problem solving*. How did he resolve the situation?"

"He woke up in the middle of the night with a brilliant idea," Lou replied. "About 25 percent of the people living in San Diego are retirees. Many retirees are bored. They'd love to have something to do, and if they could help other people, that would make it even more special. So he put an ad in the local paper that said: *Retirees: If you're good at fixing things, and you want to help people and make some extra money, give me a call.*

"It turns out he had twenty-five to thirty retirees on call every single day. So if a customer like my mother called, he had someone he could send out to her. And he didn't have the problem of a big payroll. If the people didn't work, they didn't get paid. He told me with a laugh that he had a hard time paying some of the people, because it goofed up their Social Security. They just loved the work."

"Wow, what great, out-of-the-box thinking," said Terri. "Do you have any other pointers on creating legendary service?"

"Sure," said Lou. "Tremendous Jones turned me on to Sheldon Bowles. Now his book, *Raving Fans,* is my customer-service bible. Sheldon contends there are three secrets to creating raving fan customers: decide, discover, and deliver."

"What do you mean by 'decide'?" asked Terri as she jotted some notes.

"If you want to create raving fans, you don't just announce it; you have to plan for it," said Lou. "You have to *decide* what kind of experience you want your customers to have as they interact with every aspect of your organization."

"If we're putting customers first," said Terri, "shouldn't we ask them what kind of experience they want to have?"

"Yes and no," said Lou. "While you do want input from your customers, they often don't know what the possibilities are beyond their own experience. They don't have the big picture. That's why you and your key people have to decide first what kind of experience you want your customers to have."

"How do you do that, exactly?" asked Jud.

"One of the best ideas came from Jan Carlzon, when he was president of SAS, the Scandinavian Airlines System. Carlzon used Moments of Truth as the driving-force concept for creating an ideal picture of the customer experience. He defined a Moment of Truth as 'any time a customer comes in contact with anybody in your organization in a way they can get an impression.'"

"Can you give an example of a Moment of Truth?" asked Terri.

"Sure," said Lou. "Let's take the example of a wake-up call in a hotel. What's the most common wake-up call you get in a hotel today?"

"I've been doing a lot of traveling lately," answered Jud, "so I can tell you. These days the most common wake-up call is when the phone rings, you pick it up, but there's no one there. Basically, a machine calls your room."

"Exactly," said Lou. "How about the second most common wake-up call?"

Terri said, "I've had wake-up calls where I get a recording that says something like, 'Good morning, this is your wake-up call.' But nobody's really on the line."

"It's true," said Jud. "Come to think of it, today if you pick up the phone on a wake-up call and there is a human being on the other end, you hardly know what to say!"

"Exactly," said Lou. "Here's where my example of

a Moment of Truth comes in. While I was staying at a Marriott in Orlando, the phone rang for my seven o'clock wake-up call. I picked it up and a woman said, 'Good morning, Mr. Stafford, this is Teresa. It's seven o'clock. It's going to be seventy-five degrees and beautiful in Orlando today, but your ticket says you're leaving. Where are you going?'

"I was taken aback," said Lou. "So I stammered, 'I'm going to New York City.'

"Teresa countered with, 'Let me look at the *USA Today* weather map. Oh, no! It's going to be forty degrees and rainy in New York today. Can't you stay another day?'

"Now where do you think I want to stay when I go to Orlando? I want to stay at the Marriott so I can talk to Teresa in the morning!"

"I get the picture," said Jud. "It's those little Moments of Truth that can make or break a customer relationship."

"Exactly," said Lou. "And for Carlzon and other great service providers, Moments of Truth covered every detail, including coffee stains. When he was chairman of People Express Airlines, Donald Burr contended that if the flip-down trays were dirty, customers would assume that the planes' engines were not well maintained either. When looking for a place to stay after a long day's drive, how many people would choose a motel with a sign that's missing some lights?"

"Not me," said Terri.

"While we've been talking about external customers, it's important to recognize that everyone has a customer," Lou continued. "An external customer is someone outside your organization who does business with you. A person taking orders at a quick-service restaurant is a good example of someone serving external customers. An internal customer is someone within your organization who may or may not be serving external customers. For example, people who work in the human resources field have mainly internal customers. And some people, like those in the accounting department, have both external and internal customers. They send out bills and invoices to external customers, and they provide reports and information for internal customers. The point is, everyone has a customer."

"So let me see if I get what you're saying," said Jud. "Creating legendary service starts with a picture—an image of what kind of an experience you want your customers to have. Great customer service organizations analyze every Moment of Truth they have with customers, whether they are external or internal, and determine how they would like to have that scenario played out."

"You've got it," said Lou.

"You mentioned that the second secret was 'discover,'" said Terri, glancing at her notes. "What do you mean by that?"

"After you decide what you want to have happen, it's important to discover any suggestions your customers may have that will improve their experience with your organization. What would make their experience with you better? Ask them! But ask them in a way that stimulates an answer. For example, how many times have you been eating in a restaurant when the restaurant manager comes over and says to you, 'How was everything tonight?' Isn't your usual response, 'Fine'? That gives the restaurant manager no information. A more helpful conversation would begin with, 'Excuse me. I am the restaurant manager. I wonder if I could ask you one question. Is there anything that we could have done differently tonight that would have made your experience with us better?' That question invites an answer. If the customer says 'no,' you can follow it up with a sincere, 'Are you sure?'"

"So what I'm hearing you say," said Jud, "is that if we want JTA to succeed in a big way, we're going to have to become masters of discovering what our customers are thinking. Mind readers, almost."

"You don't have to read minds, but you do have to get creative about discovering what's on your customers' minds," Lou replied. "More often than not, this requires good listening skills."

"So creating raving fan customers is just a question of listening to customers and then taking action on what you hear," said Terri, summing up.

"Yes," said Lou, "with one condition: when a customer tells you something, you have to *listen without being defensive*. One reason people get uptight when they listen to customers is that they think they always have to do what the customer wants them to do. They don't understand that there are two parts to listening. Part one is, as Steve Covey says, 'Seek first to understand.' In other words, listen for understanding. Try saying, 'That's interesting. Tell me more. Could you be more specific?'

"The second aspect of listening is deciding if you want to do anything about what you have heard," Lou continued. "That has to be separated from the understanding aspect of listening. And it is important to realize that deciding does not have to be done right after you understand what the person is suggesting. You can do it later, when you have had some time to think about it or talk it over with others. Realizing that you have time to think it over will make you less defensive and a better listener. First, listen to understand, and then decide what you want to do about what you have heard."

"I think I saw an example of defensive listening in the mall recently," Jud said. "I was walking behind a woman who had an eight- or nine-year-old son. As they walked past the sporting goods store, the kid looked over and saw a beautiful red bicycle outside the store. He stopped in his tracks and said to his mother, 'Boy, would I like a bike like that.' His mother nearly went crazy and started screaming: 'I can't believe it! I just got you a new bike for Christmas! Here it is March and you already want another one! I'm not going to get you another blankety-blank thing!' I thought she was going to nail the kid's head into the cement!"

"Sadly, that's a perfect example of someone who didn't distinguish the need to separate listening for understanding from deciding," said Lou. "If she had said to the kid, 'Honey, what do you like about the bike?' he might have said, 'You see those streamers coming out of the handlebars? I really like them.' And those streamers could have been a cheap birthday present.

"Then after listening to what he liked about the bike, the mother could have said, 'Honey, why do you think I can't get you that new bike?' The kid was no fool. He probably would have said, 'Because I just got a new bike for Christmas.'

"Listening without being defensive is also helpful if you make a mistake with a customer," continued Lou. "Defending what you have done will only irritate them. When they are upset, all customers want is to be heard. In fact, research has shown that if you listen to a complaining customer in a nondefensive, attentive way and then ask, 'Is there any way we could win back your loyalty?' eight out of ten times the customer will say, 'You have already done it. You listened to me.'

"What if a customer makes a good suggestion or is upset about something that makes sense to change?" asked Terri.

"You can add that suggestion to your customer service picture," replied Lou. "For example, recently I got a letter from a man who owns three McDonald's restaurants in the Midwest. The elderly customers from his restaurants suggested that during certain parts of the day they should have tablecloths on the tables, people taking their orders at the table, and delivering their food to the table. After thinking about it, the owner realized that this was a pretty good idea. Now, between 4:00 and 5:30 in the afternoon the tables have tablecloths and candles, and the people behind the counter come out and wait on the customers. The elderly are pouring into this restaurant during those hours.

"When you put together what you want your customers to experience with what they want to have happen, you will have a fairly complete picture of your desired customer service experience," concluded Lou. "Listening to customers, fitting their needs into your framework, and then consistently improving your level of service will turn your customers into raving fans."

"You said something earlier about 'deliver,'" said Terri, again looking at her notes. "Do you want to explain that?"

"Sure," said Lou. "It's actually deliver plus 1 percent. Once you have a clear picture of the experience you want your customers to have—an experience that will satisfy them, delight them, and put smiles on their faces—you have to figure out how to get your people excited about delivering that experience, plus a little bit more.

"The responsibility for establishing a customer service vision rests with the senior leadership. That's the *visionary* or strategic aspect of leadership. When I say 'responsibility,' that does not mean that senior leadership does not involve others, but the responsibility falls to the leadership—the top of the traditional pyramidal hierarchy. Once your desired customer service experience is set and people are committed to it, the implementation or operational aspect of leadership begins.

"It is during this implementation phase that most

organizations get into trouble," Lou continued. "The traditional pyramid is kept alive and well, leaving customers uncared for at the bottom of the hierarchy. All the energy in the organization moves up the hierarchy as people try to please and be responsive to their bosses, instead of focusing their energy on meeting the needs of their customers. Now the bureaucracy rules, and policies and procedures carry the day. This leaves unprepared and uncommitted customer contact people to quack like ducks."

"Ducks?" asked Terri.

"Yes," said Lou. "Wayne Dyer, the great personal growth teacher, said years ago there are two kinds of people in life: ducks and eagles. Ducks act like victims and go 'Quack! Quack! Quack!' Eagles, on the other hand, take initiative and soar above the crowd. As a customer, you can always identify bureaucracy if you have a problem and are confronted by ducks that quack: 'It's our policy. Quack! Quack! I didn't make the rules. Quack! Quack! I just work here. Quack! Quack! Do you want to talk to my supervisor? Quack! Quack! Quack!'

"I had a perfect example of this phenomenon when trying to rent a car," continued Lou. "I am a trustee emeritus at Cornell University. A while back I was heading to a meeting in Ithaca, New York, the small upstate town where Cornell is located. I wanted to rent a car that I could drop off at Syracuse, which was about an hour and a half away. Those who travel enough know if you drop off a car at a different place than where you rented it, the company charges a big drop-off fee. You can avoid that drop-off fee if you have a car that came from where you are going. Knowing this, I asked the woman behind the counter, 'Do you have a Syracuse car?'

"She said, 'You're lucky. I happen to have one.' Then she went into the computer and prepared my contract.

"Now I'm not a particularly detail-oriented person," said Lou with a laugh, "but as I was signing my contract, I saw a seventy-five-dollar drop-off fee out of the corner of my eye. I said, 'What's that seventy-five-dollar drop-off fee?'

"She said, 'I didn't do it. Quack! Quack!'

"I said, 'Who did?'

"She said, 'The computer. Quack! Quack!'

"I said, 'How do you tell the computer it was wrong?'

"She said, 'I don't know. Quack! Quack!'

"I said, 'Why don't you just cross it out?'

"She said, 'I can't. My boss will kill me. Quack! Quack!'

"'You mean I have to pay a seventy-five-dollar drop-off fee because you have a mean boss?' I asked.

"She said, 'I remember one time—Quack! Quack!—my boss let me cross it out.'

"'When was that?'

"'When the customer worked for Cornell,' she said. 'Quack! Quack!'

"I said, 'That's great. I'm on the Cornell Board of Trustees!'

"She asked, 'What does the board do? Quack! Quack!'

"I said, 'We can fire the president.'

"She said, 'What is your employee number? Quack! Quack!'

"'I don't have one,' I said.

"'What am I going to do? Quack! Quack!'

"It took me twenty minutes of psychological counseling to get out of this drop-off fee," Lou said. "I used to get angry with these frontline people, but don't anymore because I realize it's really not their fault.

"Who do you think this woman worked for, a duck or an eagle?" Lou asked.

"Obviously, a duck," replied Jud.

"That's right," said Lou. "If she worked for an eagle, the eagle would eat the duck. We call the supervisory duck the head mallard, because they quack higher up the hierarchy. They tell you all the rules and regulations and laws that apply to their situation. Who do you think the supervisory duck works for?"

"I'm not sure," said Jud.

"Another duck," said Lou. "And guess who that duck works for?"

"Another duck?" ventured Terri.

"That's right," said Lou. "And who sits at the top of the organization? Another great big duck. Have you ever been hit by eagle droppings? Obviously not, because eagles soar above the crowd. It's the ducks that make all the mess."

"How do you create an organization where ducks are busted and eagles can soar?" asked Jud.

"That's where I think you ought to talk to one of

your board advisors for JTA, Nancy Kaline. As Nancy can tell you, the way to create eagles is to treat your people as partners so they feel empowered to act like they own the place. Nancy knows more about partnering with your people than anyone I've ever met."

"Sounds great, Lou," said Jud. "Thanks for all your help."

After talking to Lou, Jud and Terri shared with all their people about Moments of Truth. They asked each department to analyze all the touch points they had with their customers and to decide how they wanted those touch points to be played out. When everyone had done that, they gathered together for a service excellence day and inspired each other with the results of their work.

One Minute Insights

☞ Analyzing your Moments of Truth can help you decide the kind of experience you want your customers to have.

☞ Truly listening to your customers and discovering their ideas can make your vision even better.

☞ Duck busting is sometimes necessary before people can soar like eagles and deliver your customer service vision.

Helping People Soar Like Eagles

Jud, Terri, and Jeremy were excited to meet with Nancy Kaline and hear her ideas on how they could help their people to soar like eagles. Nancy had taken over the presidency of her large, family-owned company from her father, who had built an incredible business from scratch, with a classic "my way or the highway" leadership style. Yet that hadn't seemed to work in the last few years of his reign.

"Several things changed," said Nancy. "First of all, business is much more complicated today than when my dad started. Globalization, intense competition, and rapid and constant technological change were stretching him beyond his comfort zone. The one-man-band strategy of decision making just didn't cut it anymore. Today's knowledge workers want a partnership relationship with their leaders."

"Partnership?" said Jud.

"Yes," said Nancy. "People today believe the leadership needs them as much as they need the leadership. If they don't feel valued or involved, they will go elsewhere in a flash. Just like the customers of today, loyalty from your people has to be earned."

"How do you earn people's loyalty?" Terri wondered aloud.

"By letting people bring their brains to work, so— as Lou would say—they can soar like eagles instead of quack like ducks," said Nancy. "To do that requires bosses who are servant leaders."

"When I hear the term 'servant leadership,'" said Jud, "it sounds like the inmates are running the prison, or you're trying to please everyone."

"Or some kind of religious movement, right?" said Nancy with a laugh. "To truly understand what servant leadership is all about, you have to recognize there are two aspects of leadership: vision and implementation. I'm sure Lou talked to you about that. The visionary aspect of leadership sets the direction, the values, and the major business initiatives. That's the 'lead' part of servant leadership. It's all about strategic leadership. This is what my father was good at."

"It sounds like he was a big-picture guy," said Terri.

"He sure was," said Nancy with a smile. "And he had a number of experienced folks who were with him from the beginning, who would do anything to please him and make things happen. They were the typical employees of the past. They were hardwired to be loyal and do what they were told. Without folks like them, Dad would have been in trouble. He didn't focus much on implementation. He was not an operational guy. He would set the direction and then expect that what he wanted to have happen, would happen."

"What do you mean?" asked Jeremy.

"He would tell people what the task was, and then he'd disappear," said Nancy. "In many ways he would abdicate and head off looking for the next business opportunity. He would only return if something was wrong, and then he'd swoop in like a seagull, make a lot of noise, dump on everybody, and then fly out."

"You've got to have real loyal people to tolerate that leadership style, don't you?" asked Terri.

"That's for sure," said Nancy. "When I took over the leadership, most of these folks were retiring or heading that way. It's a whole new ballgame now. Sure, people know that all good performance starts with clear goals, but what interests them the most is *how* those goals are going to be accomplished—the operational leadership. That's where the 'servant' part of servant leadership comes in."

"Tell us more," said Terri.

"Today people think that leadership is not something you do to them, but something you do with them," continued Nancy. "Since they want to win—accomplish the goals—they want managers who will work with them to make that happen. They want leaders who think of them as partners. They want servant leaders."

"I recently read," said Jud, "that people who produce good results feel good about themselves."

"That's well said," responded Nancy. "Leadership that positively impacts both performance and satisfaction is how healthy, productive organizations are created and sustained. Unfortunately, many leaders, including entrepreneurs, do not provide the kind of leadership that nurtures both performance *and* satisfaction."

"How can we as entrepreneurs make sure that we are emphasizing both people and results?" asked Jud.

"As I've said, the best way I know is to focus on leadership as a partnership relationship with your people," said Nancy. "In most organizations, leadership is commonly thought of in a hierarchical context, where the leader is in charge of the team members. That kind of leadership does not bring out the best in people."

"What I hear you saying," said Jud, "is that leadership that is perceived as side by side rather than top to bottom is more likely to create high performance and satisfaction."

"That's right," said Nancy. "With this side-by-side partnership, the focus is on helping people produce good results so they can feel good about themselves and the organization can win."

Now Nancy really had Jud and Terri's attention.

"One of the outcomes of such a partnership is that it encourages everyone to become a leader. Entrepreneurs who keep their people do just that. They realize that they can't do everything by themselves and they have to depend on the people they hire to take their dream, run with it, and make things happen. If mistakes are made, these leaders use these occasions as learning opportunities, rather than as a time to punish and downgrade others."

"I see a lot of entrepreneurs who let their egos eat their brains," said Jud. "They start to think their business is all about them and forget about the importance of their people. I certainly fell into that trap."

"Led by Forrest," interjected Terri. "And that's why we got in trouble."

"It's an easy trap to fall into," said Nancy. "But if your organization is all about you, today people will not be committed to your dream. They'll shuffle in and out of your organization, depending on good offers elsewhere. When you think of your people as your partners, they'll begin to act like they own the place. And that is exactly what you want them to do."

"How do you make people your partners, exactly?" asked Jeremy.

"You have to set up a good performance management system," Nancy replied.

"The word 'system' often has a negative connotation," said Jud with a smile.

"You're right," said Nancy. "Most entrepreneurs don't think of organizing their people management into a system. Yet as Peter Drucker often said, 'Nothing good happens by accident.' I am sure you have several people in your life who always remember your birthday."

They all nodded.

"They are very thoughtful people," continued Nancy. "How do you think they became so thoughtful? They are organized. They have some system that signals them several weeks before your birthday that it is coming up. That same kind of systematic thinking has to drive your management of people."

"What does a good performance management system involve?" asked Jud.

"There are three parts to an effective performance management system," said Nancy. "The first is *performance planning*. This is when you agree with your people about the goals and objectives that they should be focusing their energy on. As we've said, all good performance starts with clear goals."

"So if people don't know where they are going, they have little chance of getting there," said Terri with a smile.

"That's for sure," said Nancy. "That's why throughout most organizations people get punished for not doing what they didn't know they were supposed to do in the first place."

"So goal setting helps eliminate that," said Jud.

"It certainly helps," said Nancy. "Particularly if people not only know what they are being asked to do, but they also know what good performance looks like—what the performance standards are."

"Does the partnering for performance relationship begin with performance planning?" asked Terri.

"Yes," said Nancy, "but you have to remember that during performance planning, it's okay for the traditional hierarchy to be alive and well, because if there is a disagreement between a manager and a direct report about goals, who wins?"

"The manager, I assume," said Terri.

"Yes," replied Nancy, "because that person represents the goals and objectives of the total organization. That doesn't mean that you don't involve your people in goal setting, particularly experienced ones. It just means, as I've said before, that the responsibility for goal setting getting done rests with the manager. This is the 'lead' aspect of servant leadership."

"What's the second aspect of a good performance review system?" asked Jud.

"It's *day-to-day coaching*," said Nancy. "This is

where you invert the pyramid and turn the hierarchy upside down."

"Why do you do that?" asked Jeremy.

"Because now the manager becomes the cheerleader and supporter of all good performance by his or her people," said Nancy. "It's the role of the manager here to do everything he or she can do to help team members be successful. This is where the partnering relationship and the 'serve' aspect of servant leadership really kick in. Now the manager is doing everything he or she can to help team members soar like eagles."

"What's the third aspect of an effective performance management system?" asked Jud.

"It's *performance evaluation*," said Nancy. "This is where managers and their direct reports sit down and examine the performance of the team member over time."

"I used to dread performance evaluation sessions," said Jud, "even though I knew Dirk was on my side."

"The reason most people dread their performance evaluation sessions," said Nancy, "is they are never quite sure how they will be evaluated. They just hope they have a good relationship with their boss and, therefore, that their evaluation will go well."

"That certainly was the way it was with me," said Jud. "I know Dirk had some form he had filled out on me."

"Oh, yes, the form," said Nancy. "When I go into most organizations, people will say to me, 'You're going to love our new performance evaluation form.' I always laugh, because I think that most of them can be thrown out."

"Why do you say that?" said Terri.

"Because these forms often measure things that nobody knows how to evaluate. For example, 'initiative' or 'willingness to take responsibility.' Or 'promotability'—that's a good one.

"When no one knows how to win on an evaluation form," continued Nancy, "they focus most of their energy up the hierarchy. After all, as Jud said, if you have a good relationship with your boss, you have a higher probability of getting a good evaluation."

"That really rings a bell with me," said Jud, "because I never knew exactly how Dirk was going to evaluate me, except with my sales numbers, which were very specific."

"That gets back to performance standards, Jud," said Nancy. "Remember I said that all good performance starts with clear goals, and you need performance standards? Remember, if you can't measure something, you can't manage it. Often people are evaluated on unclear areas, where they don't even know what good performance looks like. And sometimes they haven't even been told that their boss is interested in that area."

"Let me get back to goal setting for a minute," said Terri. "Don't most organizations do a pretty good job on goal setting?"

"Yes, they do," replied Nancy, "but unfortunately after setting goals, what do you think happens to those goals in most cases?"

Jud started to laugh. "I bet they get filed."

"You got it," said Nancy. "And no one looks at them until they are told, 'It's time for performance review.' Now everybody is running around bumping into each other, trying to find the goals."

"So the goals are not used actively during the year?" Terri said.

"No, they're not," replied Nancy.

"Why?" said Jud.

"Let me answer the question by asking you a question," said Nancy. "Of the three aspects of an effective performance management system, what's the one on which the least time is spent?"

"I know it's not performance evaluation," said Jud with a laugh, "because that seems to me to be the one aspect of what you're talking about that every manager focuses on."

"I bet it's day-to-day coaching," said Terri.

"Bingo!" said Nancy. "The least amount of time that managers spend is on coaching, yet this is the most important aspect of managing people's performance. It's here where feedback—praising progress and redirecting inappropriate behavior—moves to center stage. This is where your manager is really your partner, because he or she is giving you feedback on your goals and the results you are getting."

"I've heard that feedback is the breakfast of champions," said Jeremy.

"It sure is," said Nancy. "If you want people to win and accomplish their goals, then they need somebody observing and monitoring their behavior after goals are established. Now is when you guide them in the right direction if they are off base, and praise and cheer them on if they are on the money."

"This is really exciting stuff," said Jud.

"I'm glad you think so," said Nancy, "because it's all-important. To illustrate what I've been talking about, let me share with you a story about a college professor I had. He was always in trouble. He was investigated by some of the best faculty committees. What drove the faculty crazy more than anything was that at the beginning of every class he gave students the final exam. When the faculty found out about that, they'd say, 'What are you doing?'

"Not knowing why they were questioning him, he'd say, 'I'm confused.'

"They'd say, 'You act like it.'

"He'd say, 'I thought we were supposed to teach these students.'

"The faculty would say, 'You are, but don't give the students the final exam ahead of time.'

"He'd say, 'Not only am I going to give them the final exam ahead of time—what do you think I am going to do throughout the semester? I'm going to teach them the answers, so that when they get to the final exam, they get As. You see, life is all about getting As, not some stupid normal distribution curve.'"

"What a great philosophy," said Jud.

"It is," said Nancy. "He impacted my leadership point of view significantly. Do you two ever go out and hire losers? Do you go around saying, 'We lost some of our best losers last year, so let's go out and hire some new ones to fill those low slots'?"

"I sure hope we don't!" said Terri. "I'd like to think we go out and hire either winners or potential winners."

"So you don't hire people to fit a normal distribution curve, do you?" said Nancy.

"Absolutely not," said Terri.

"So you want to be careful that you don't fall into that trap, whether it's officially or unofficially," continued Nancy. "So often managers think of their job as judging, evaluating, and criticizing their people, rather than helping, cheerleading, and supporting their efforts."

"I hear what you're saying loud and clear," said Jud.

"Giving people the final exam ahead of time is equivalent to performance planning," continued Nancy. "Now they know exactly what's expected of them. Teaching people the answers is what day-to-day coaching is all about. If you see somebody doing something right, you give them an 'atta boy' or 'atta girl.' If they do something wrong, you don't beat them up. You just say, 'Wrong answer. What do you think would be the right answer?' In other words, you redirect them. And at the end of the performance period, giving people the same 'exam' you gave them at the beginning of the 'semester' makes the performance evaluation more effective."

"So you're saying there should be no surprises at an annual or semiannual performance evaluation," said Jeremy.

"That's exactly what I'm saying," said Nancy.

"Everyone should know what the test is going to be, and that they are going to get help throughout the year to achieve a high score. When you have a forced distribution where a certain percentage of your people have to lose, you lose everyone's trust. Now all they are concerned about is looking out for number one."

"I like the philosophy you've been sharing, Nancy," said Jud. "Are there any organizations you've seen that are really using it?"

"Yes," said Nancy, "particularly if their top management is enlightened. For example, I read recently that Garry Ridge, president of WD-40, has implemented 'Don't Mark My Paper—Help Me Get an A' as the major theme in his company. He is so emphatic about this belief and the kind of performance management system that I've been talking about that he fired the manager of a poor performer rather than the poor performer, because that manager had done nothing to help the poor performer get an A. In his organization, he wants everyone to know that the management of people is a partnership relationship that helps people get As."

"What if you work closely with someone and they still don't deserve an A?" asked Terri.

"Then don't give it to them," said Nancy. "But recognize that they're probably in the wrong job. Now you move to career planning."

"We give in," said Jud. "We get what you're talking about. If we want our people to soar like eagles and take care of our customers, we have to create an environment where they can win—where they know that we're on their side—so they will be empowered to act like they own the place."

"That's it," said Nancy. "Leadership that emphasizes judgment, criticism, and evaluation is a relic of the past. Effective leadership for an entrepreneur today is about treating people the right way by providing the direction and encouragement they need to be their best. If you help your people get As, then you have a performance management system that will ignite them to blow your customers away, because they feel good about themselves and want to return the favor to others."

"So it sounds like there's a real payoff for what you've been teaching us," said Jud.

"There sure is," said Nancy. "If you treat your people right, they get passionate about their work and your organization. Their passion overflows to your customers as they go out of the way to serve them well. Your customers feel that passion and experience great service, and end up being loyal to your organization. Loyal customers tell stories about your organization and are complimentary about your people. Your good reputation begins to spread like a prairie fire on a windy day! That re-motivates your people, and together, it's passionate people and loyal customers who really bring success to your organization. The vision and strategic direction start it off, but how goals are accomplished and strategies are implemented is where the partnership relationship comes into play."

"We can't thank you enough," said Jud, "for all your help. When it comes to taking care of our people, we've got plenty of great ideas to work on now."

One Minute Insights

☞ Today people want a partnership relationship, not a superior-subordinate relationship.

☞ Encourage everyone to become a leader.

☞ An effective performance management system helps people win rather than sorts them out.

☞ The best management includes day-to-day coaching that catches people doing things right and redirects their efforts when they are off base.

☞ Life is all about getting As.

☞ Passionate people and loyal customers are what really bring success to your organization.

Putting It All Together

Jud and Terri, with yeoman help from Jeremy, spent the next several years putting into action all they had learned from Red and Juan about finances, as well as Lou and Nancy's advice about delivering legendary service and helping their people soar like eagles. The results outshone their brightest hopes.

Jeremy did a great job of implementing the recommendations from the task forces organized by Jud and Terri to study how to cut costs. He constantly reinforced the need for everyone in the organization to know how important it was for sales to exceed expenses and to reduce accounts receivable. He realized you can't cost-cut your way to prosperity. But he emphasized that everyone had to use good judgment and stay on top of the finances.

On the sales side, Jeremy pressed everyone, not just salespeople, to ramp up their efforts to pursue opportunities that could lead to increased sales. What impressed everyone was that Jeremy served as a good role model.

Jeremy found a new revenue stream when he contacted a college friend who had become the CEO of LJF Corporation, one of the nation's largest food-service companies. Matt Rhoads was doing an excellent job running the company, but he realized that they now had a much bigger opportunity than his trained workforce could handle. To close the gap between

LJF's potential and performance, Jeremy worked closely with Matt to spearhead the formation of "LJF University."

The "university platform" provided numerous valuable functions, one of the most powerful being the intrepreneurship program, which inspired employees to take ownership of new initiatives and get their people to buy in. It was essentially a concept of promoting innovative, entrepreneurial thinking in a corporate environment. All components of it were taught on the company's intranet platform created by JTA. After interviewing several of their key people at LJF, Jeremy and Jud—with input from Lou—created a successful program for them based on ten principles:

1. Companies must constantly innovate. Without innovation they tend to do what they've always done and run the risk of getting stale and thus competitively disadvantaged.

2. For a company to thrive it must tap the individual initiative of team members. This must be a major area of focus.

3. On any initiative being pursued, team member buy-in is absolutely essential for success.

4. If a company wants its people to be intrepreneurial in their thinking,

they must be kept well informed about processes and visions—and their impact on profit and loss.

5. Leaders must give all team members everything they need to succeed and be self-motivated.

6. Companies must reward the creativity of their people.

7. If a team member owns an initiative, he or she should be accountable for all aspects of its success.

8. Companies must encourage resourcefulness and out-of-the-box thinking.

9. All thought leaders must be constantly focused on customer needs and how to satisfy and exceed them.

10. Leaders and managers must work to maximize team member involvement in all key initiatives to tap the collective intellect of the team.

When Jeremy presented the guidelines to Matt at LJF, he encouraged him to put together a company task force of four or five forward-thinking leaders who could dig deeper into each point to make sure it would be a good fit for LJF.

"Anytime you can give key people opportunities for authorship, they will buy in with greater resolve and determination," Jeremy said.

The game plan worked, and the food-service company started growing by leaps and bounds. Matt Rhoads attributed the enhanced revenues and profits to the initiative JTA had formulated for them and the close working relationship he had developed with Jeremy Britton. As a result, JTA also grew—a lot.

When it came to creating legendary service, every department at JTA continued to identify their Moments of Truth with customers and to focus on delivering their ideal customer service vision.

To reinforce everyone's attempts to create raving fan customers, Jud, Terri, and Jeremy decided to eliminate the Employee of the Month Program, which had been part of the JTA culture for years. In its place they substituted an Employee of the Moment Program. Anytime someone was seen—either by an external or an internal customer—as going beyond the call of duty to serve that customer, there was an immediate celebration. An eagle's nest was established, where associates were armed with cameras and ready to photograph eagles in flight. A Wall of Fame was created where stories and pictures of JTA associates caught creating raving fan customers were displayed. There were no restrictions on how many times a person could appear on the Wall of Fame.

To help people soar like eagles, the JTA performance management system was transformed into a partnering for performance system. Every manager was taught coaching essentials so they could establish clear goals and performance standards, praise progress, and redirect efforts that were off the mark. Managing by Wandering Around became a way of life. Managers were expected to have one-on-one meetings with each of their direct reports every two weeks. These meetings only lasted between fifteen and thirty minutes, but permitted direct reports to update their managers on their progress and ask for any additional help that might be needed. This kept both members of the partnership—manager and direct report—up-to-date.

As a result, when it came to performance reviews, there was no new news. These end-of-year discussions were really a review of all the things that the partners—managers and their direct reports—had been talking about all year long. The goal of every partnership was to empower people to be problem solvers, not subordinates waiting for superiors to tell them what to do.

All these efforts produced not only great financial results, but a work environment that was the envy of other companies. When Jud and Terri looked at the year-end numbers, they had the same thought.

"Remember three years ago when we said we'd take everyone to Hawaii after we pulled out of the financial hole we were in?" said Jud. "I think the time has come."

"I agree!" said Terri.

Jeremy agreed as well, and the plans were set. In February, 150 JTA associates—including some spouses—headed to Maui for a four-day celebration of the company's turnaround. On the last evening a fabulous band was hired to play at a farewell luau. Everyone danced barefoot in the sand and had a ball. At the end of the evening the leader of the band was so blown away by the energy of the group that he looked down from the stage and said, "I don't know what you guys do for a living, but keep it up. You've got to be doing something right!"

With JTA back on its feet, Jud and Terri turned some of their energy to their own finances. This was a response to some priceless advice from Tremendous.

"Now that you have stopped the bleeding at JTA, it would be a good time to begin focusing on your personal dollars and your future financial dreams," said Tremendous.

"Tell us more," said Jud and Terri, almost in unison.

"During the financial crisis you just went through, you learned how important good banking relationships are," said Tremendous.

"We sure did," said Jud. "Even though we had good relationships during our hard times, they still asked for a personal guarantee for the company's credit line."

"So you were under the gun for the performance of the company?" said Tremendous.

"We sure were," said Terri. "The turnaround has helped us sleep better, because all our money was tied up in the company."

"One of the things that saved you both was that you didn't suffer from the 'I need' disease that afflicts so many people," said Tremendous. "They buy too much lifestyle, and then their net worth shows minimal growth."

"What, exactly, is net worth?" asked Terri.

"Your personal net worth," said Tremendous, "is your assets minus liabilities or debt. If you don't delay gratification and keep spending all the time, your net worth will grow slowly, if at all."

"It sounds like a personal version of our old friend: sales must exceed expenses," said Jud with a laugh. "If we are to grow our personal net worth, our income has to exceed our expenses."

"Absolutely," said Tremendous. "You have to watch your 'lifestyle costs.'"

"What's the best way to do that?" asked Terri.

"Planning," said Tremendous. "The best advice Gloria and I ever heard was early in our marriage. Our pastor advised us to put 10 percent of our income into a savings account every month and then give another 10 percent away to charities and other nonprofit organizations. He told us we had to learn how to live on 80 percent of our income."

"So you believe in tithing?" asked Jud.

"I certainly do," said Tremendous. "I once heard Sir John Templeton, one of the great financial investors of our time, speak. He told everyone that the best financial advice he'd ever given anyone was to tithe. He argued that you should not wait until you have all kinds of money before you tithe. Make it a monthly habit, no matter how low your income is."

"That's interesting," said Terri.

"Templeton said he's never known anyone who had tithed at least 10 percent of their income for ten years," continued Tremendous, "who didn't have what they gave away coming back to them tenfold. When you reach out to help others, you invariably get more back in return."

"That's something we should start to do, then," said Jud. "Is that what you're recommending?"

"It's your decision," said Tremendous with a smile. "Remember, this is priceless advice. But this has to do with the last thing I learned from Sheldon Bowles in *Big Bucks*."

"I certainly remember *play to your passion* and finding people who will *pay for your passion*. If you don't do what you love, you'll never work hard enough to be the best. But remember: if you don't find people who will pay you to do what you love, you have a hobby, not a career," said Jud.

"You've gotten those two right with JTA," said Tremendous. "But do you remember *plus your passion*?"

"Oh yes," said Jud. "You have to find ways to create new income streams that build off what you are already passionate about."

"You certainly have done a good job on those three things individually and with your organization," said Tremendous. "You have a lot of people who love what they do and are getting paid to do it. And you have been creative and resourceful in finding new ways to earn income that are an outgrowth of your speaking business."

"Thanks for noticing," said Jud with a smile. "Now

stop stalling. What's the last thing you learned from Sheldon?"

"It's all about what we've been talking about: *pass on the prosperity* from your passion. That's what Sheldon calls the test of perpetual prosperity. He and I agree that you'll never really be successful unless you help others. Helping others does not just involve the financial gains from your prosperity, but also includes sharing your time and talent. Mentoring others is a way to pass on what you've gotten from others along the way."

This whole conversation made Jud very reflective. He felt he had come full circle. From a broke kid out of college with lots of ambition he had become a successful entrepreneur. Yet in some ways he was still unfulfilled. It made him think deeply about the fragility of life and the more important issues, like leaving a legacy that could positively impact others.

Noticing the thoughtful look on Jud's face, Tremendous said, "What's on your mind?"

"I was thinking about what kind of legacy Terri and I can leave."

"Interesting you should mention that," said Tremendous. "I was reading a wonderful book by Bob Buford called *Halftime* the other day. He argues that at some point in all of our lives we want to move from success to significance—from getting to giving. I think that's what a legacy is all about."

"That's certainly where Terri and I are right now," said Jud.

"Everyone leaves a legacy," said Tremendous,

"whether they intend to or not. People who are more intentional about it usually leave a better legacy behind. Everything you are and possess today, good or bad, will pass down to those who come after you—not only the monetary stuff, but also your beliefs and philosophy."

"How can Terri and I be more intentional about the legacy we leave?" asked Jud.

"You have to learn what real prosperity is," said Tremendous. "Riches aren't a fixed pie that gets divided up with only so much to go around. Riches constantly grow by supplying goods and services to others. In the process, you either add value to whatever is already there or you create something new. When you help others realize their potential, you may well be turning a horse and buggy into a jet plane! The result is a whole new pie of riches, and some of the slices will probably come back to you. As I mentioned earlier, when you reach out to help someone else, you often get more back in return. It's about having a spirit of abundance rather than scarcity."

That conversation with Tremendous focused Jud and Terri on helping and giving back to others. It played out in their company in two ways. First, they started a gain-sharing program, where they took 10 percent of their profit every year and shared it equally with all of their people. Every month the balance sheet was shared, so everyone knew how well they were doing and what it would take to increase everyone's share of the pie.

They also took another 10 percent of their profit and gave it back to employees to tithe to charity causes of their own choosing. The only requirement was that the charity had 501(c) tax status and that they did not give to the general fund, but to a specific project. This made sure people really found out about their charity.

They also started JTA for Others, a nonprofit group that people could contribute to with monthly paycheck deductions and various fund-raising activities. The charities that JTA for Others focused on were chosen by the employees. The donations went to a wide range of worthy causes, including hurricane relief, environmental preservation, aid to the needy, medical care for those in financial crisis, and plane tickets for associates who needed to be with faraway loved ones who were sick or hurting.

The head of HR was given an "angel fund" to disperse among associates when circumstances deemed it necessary. Jud would leave global voicemail messages when somebody was hurting and ask for love and prayers to be sent their way. JTA truly became a family organization, in more ways than one.

Tremendous was right. When you give to others, it comes back to you in spades. JTA continued to grow and thrive over the years. It was chosen one of the best companies to work for and in the process attracted Alex and Elizabeth's attention, because by this time they both had graduated from college and were out in the workforce. Alex had attended a hotel school and was working in the hospitality industry. Elizabeth, who had always been a fashion plate, was working in the retail apparel industry.

When Jud and Terri, who were more in love now than ever before, realized their kids might be interested in joining their company, they decided to form a family council. It would include both of them, Alex and Elizabeth, and Jeremy, who had become like a family member and was now the president and COO of the company. They hired a consultant, Jim Elder, who had been working with family businesses for over twenty years, to meet with them for a minimum of one day a quarter.

When Jim Elder began working with the family, he started off by individually interviewing each of the five members of the family council. Finally, he came to Terri and Jud.

"I'm going to ask you the toughest question that the founders of a family business have to answer. Do you want Alex, Elizabeth, and Jeremy to be owners of the company, regardless of whether they ever work in it?"

"Why do you ask that?" said Jud.

"Because one of the biggest problems I have seen with family businesses is that family members and close friends take on positions in the organization that they are not qualified to hold, just to protect their ownership. Ownership and management position should be two separate things. If Jeremy, Alex, and Elizabeth become owners, they should be paid ownership benefits regardless of their involvement in the company. If Alex and Elizabeth decide to take management positions, they should be paid a fair-market salary for that responsibility, over and above any ownership shares. This tends to focus everybody's energy on how they can best contribute to the success of the organization. No matter what they do, even if it is nothing, their ownership is protected."

That's exactly what Jud and Terri decided to do. In the beginning, they gradually turned over 19.5 percent ownership each to Alex and Elizabeth and 10 percent to Jeremy. But over time, when everyone realized what a long-term partner Jeremy was, the kids came to Jud and Terri and argued for equal status for Jeremy. Eventually all five members of the family council owned 20 percent of the company.

Alex turned out to be a chip off the old man's block and became a great speaker and cheerleader for the company. Elizabeth, like her mom, was better suited for a managerial position, and she soon became head of sales.

As Jud and Terri began approaching their fortieth anniversary, they smiled and reflected back on how far this whole entrepreneurial adventure had come. They knew it would never have been possible without all of the mentors who had come into their lives.

"In many ways, my life started to take a positive turn with Race Nelson," said Jud to Terri with a laugh. "When I got caught in Race's car with marijuana, I thought it was the end of the world. Now I'm grateful for what happened, because I learned so much from it. I'm convinced it changed my life. In a way, Race was my first mentor."

"I'd vote for Dirk Gardner," said Terri. "After all, he launched your speaking and sales career."

"He sure did," said Jud. "But the best mentor of all is the ever available and endearing Charlie Tremendous Jones, who brought us together. He always seems to have the right advice at the right time."

They continued to reminisce about the people who had impacted their entrepreneurship the most. They would never forget Tremendous's friend, Harris Palmer, who gave them fundamental advice:

- Sales have to exceed expenses
- Collect your bills
- Take care of your customers
- Take care of your people

Red O'Rourke and Juan Escobar had certainly reinforced the importance of CASH, CASH, CASH. Lou Stafford had made them realize that legendary service was a choice that started with Moments of Truth and continued with a philosophy of leading by listening. Nancy Kaline had taught them that your people are not your subordinates; they are your partners, and you can't expect people to take care of your customers if you don't create an environment where they can bring their brains to work and act like owners.

As they reviewed all their learnings, Jud and Terri committed not only to continue to mentor, together with Jeremy, their wonderful kids Alex and Elizabeth, but also to reach out to help other young people who had the guts to take advantage of the wonderful free enterprise system that was the foundation of their country. They wanted to encourage those who were willing to step out and take a risk to become entrepreneurs.

They laughed to themselves as they realized that

once a commitment to be an entrepreneur is made, it's one step at a time.

"Remember when Tremendous told us we had to substitute strategic patience for crisis management?" asked Terri.

"Yes," said Jud. "He said we were doing all the right things. We just needed to keep doing them one day at a time."

"Some days, it felt more like one minute at a time," Terri recalled with a laugh.

"You're right about that," said Jud. It's the moment-to-moment and minute-to-minute decisions you make every day that turn you into a successful entrepreneur."

"You know what that makes us, don't you?" asked Terri with a wink.

"No," said Jud, "but I have a feeling you're going to tell me."

"One Minute Entrepreneurs, of course!"

One Minute Insights

☞ For great joy in life, be generous with your wealth, time, and talent.

☞ Giving can be much more enjoyable than receiving.

☞ We all leave legacies. Be intentional about yours.

☞ It is impossible to out-give yourself.

☞ You never know the good that can come from helping or forgiving someone.

Appendix: Entrepreneur Attributes

 | **Top 20 Attributes of Successful Entrepreneurs**

Listed below are the top 20 attributes of a successful entrepreneur that were highlighted in the book:

1. *Resourceful*
2. *Purposeful*
3. *Focus*
4. *Risk taker*
5. *Problem solver*
6. *Salesmanship*
7. *Visionary*
8. *Optimistic*
9. *Leadership*
10. *Ambitious*
11. *Innovative*
12. *Integrity*
13. *Adaptable*
14. *Communicator*
15. *Self-motivation*
16. *Strategist*
17. *Team*
18. *Determination*
19. *Curious*
20. *Balance*

Go to **www.estrengths.com** to take a **free assessment** and see how you measure up in each key attribute.

Acknowledgments

A book like this doesn't get written by the authors alone. Mentors like Charlie Tremendous Jones and Sheldon Bowles come into your life to help impact your thinking. We have continued to learn wonderful insights about life and work from great speakers and authors like Ken McFarland, Bill Gove, Zig Ziglar, Peter Drucker, Denis Waitley, Brian Tracy, Stephen Covey, Harvey Mackay, Patrick Lencioni, Wayne Dyer, Jim Collins, Jim Rohn, Suze Orman, Tom Peters, Tom Landry, Phil Hodges, Rabbi Harold Kushner, and Jan Carlzon.

Ken would never be where he is today if it weren't for the mentoring he got from Paul Hersey. Their relationship goes back to the sixties, when they were teaching at Ohio University, and continues today as they collaborate and compete with each other's entrepreneurial companies in Escondido, California.

First we want to acknowledge Ethan Willis and Randy Garn from Prosper, Inc., and Tom McKee and Kevin Small from The Ken Blanchard Companies, who encouraged us to write this book. Without their gentle shove, this manuscript might never have come to fruition.

Second, without expert writers better than us, we would have been lost, particularly Martha Lawrence, Ken's writing partner and inspiration. Susan Drake, Jonellen Heckler, and Dr. Terry Paulson, colleagues of Don's, added invaluable editorial assistance.

Special thanks also go to people who read the manuscript and were willing to give us feedback. They include Kemmons Wilson Jr., Jerry Britton, Beverly Britton, Joe Hensley, Ruth Ann Hensley, L. D. Beard, Sondra Fondren, Mark Ruleman, Frank Colvett Sr., Earl Blankenship, Frank Watson Jr., Dr. Paul Green, David Waddell, Scott Messmore, Joan Messmore, Greg Casals, Phil Donovan, Steve Williford, Bentley Goodwin, Chris Mercer, Jerry Cardwell, Petie Parker, Pat Kandel, Carmela Southers, Jan Nast-Carter, Martha Maher, Linda Hulst, Gwin Scott, Jr., and Terri Murphy.

Ken and Margie Blanchard are indebted to a number of entrepreneurs who went out of their way to help them during the infant stages of The Ken Blanchard Companies. They include Dick Pratt, entrepreneur extraordinaire who heads up the largest company in Australia, who was the first to give them the four keys to being a successful entrepreneur. Red Scott from San Diego emphasized the importance of cash, cash, cash. Advice from John Anderson from Illinois, Peter Meinig from Oklahoma, John Metz from Pennsylvania, Alan Raffee from California, and Dick Reiten from Oregon—who formed the original advisory board for their company— was invaluable as Ken and Margie launched their entrepreneurial career. Garry Ridge, another Australian and president of WD-40, practices everything we preach.

Don acknowledges the late Dick Gardner, his early mentor and insightful manager, who gave him his first job out of college.

Special thanks to Richard Andrews for all his help

on our contracts, which has permitted this book to become a reality. Special thanks also go to three organizations that have impacted us both. The Young Presidents' Organization (YPO), the National Speakers Association (NSA), and Toastmasters International. All three of these organizations are full of cheerleaders and encouragers for people who want to make a difference in the world.

Last but not least, thanks to our wives Margie and Terri, who permitted us to marry above ourselves and become better human beings in the process. They are important entrepreneurial partners for us today.

Selected Readings

By Ken Blanchard

The One Minute Manager (with Spencer Johnson)

Leadership and the One Minute Manager (with Drea Zigarmi and Pat Zigarmi)

Self Leadership and the One Minute Manager (with Susan Fowler and Laurence Hawkins)

The Generosity Factor (with Truett Cathy)

Leading at a Higher Level: Blanchard on Leadership and Creating High Performing Organizations (with the Founding Associates and Consulting Partners of The Ken Blanchard Companies)

Whale Done! The Power of Positive Relationships (with Jim Ballard, Chuck Tompkins, and Thad Lacinak)

By Don Hutson

The Contented Achiever: How to Get What You Want and Love What You Get (with Chris Couch and George Lucas)

Speaking Secrets of the Masters (with the members of Speakers Roundtable)

Insights into Excellence (with the members of Speakers Roundtable)

Taking Charge: Lessons in Leadership (anthology)

The Sale: 25 High-Performance Selling Skills to Master Before Your Competitors Do

By Sheldon Bowles

Raving Fans: A Revolutionary Approach to Customer Service (with Ken Blanchard)

Gung Ho! Turn On the People in Any Organization (with Ken Blanchard)

Big Bucks! How to Make Serious Money for Both You and Your Company (with Ken Blanchard)

Kingdomality: An Ingenious New Way to Triumph in Management (with Richard Silvano and Susan Silvano)

By Charlie Tremendous Jones

Life Is Tremendous

Humor Is Tremendous

Quotes Are Tremendous

Forgiveness Is Tremendous

Books Are Tremendous

The Books You Read: 4 Volumes

Four Star Leadership for Leaders

The Tremendous Power of Prayer

By Michael Gerber

The E-Myth

The E-Myth Revisited: Why Most Small Businesses Don't Work and What to Do about It

E-Myth Mastery: The Seven Essential Disciplines for Building a World-Class Company

About the Authors

Ken Blanchard has had an extraordinary impact on the day-to-day management of millions of people and companies. He is the author of several best-selling books, including the blockbuster international bestseller *The One Minute Manager*® and the giant business bestsellers *Leadership and the One Minute Manager, Raving Fans,* and *Gung Ho!* His books have combined sales of more than 18 million copies in more than twenty-five languages. In 2005 Ken was inducted into Amazon's Hall of Fame as one of the top twenty-five best-selling authors of all time.

Ken is the chief spiritual officer of The Ken Blanchard Companies, an international management training and consulting firm. He is also cofounder of the Lead Like Jesus Ministries, a nonprofit organization dedicated to inspiring and equipping people to be servant leaders in the marketplace.

Don Hutson of Memphis, Tennessee, is CEO of U.S. Learning. He has given over five thousand speeches in twenty-two countries in the past thirty-five years and is in the National Speakers Association's Speakers Hall of Fame. Don was on the founding board of the National Speakers Association, served as its third president, and received the Cavett Award as Member of the Year. He is on the board of directors of the Society of Entrepreneurs and served as its president.

Don Hutson is author or coauthor of nine books, including *The Sale* and *The Contented Achiever*, and has published his sales and management training programs on CD and DVD. He is featured regularly on both PBS and TSTN Television.

Ethan Willis of South Pasadena, California, is cofounder and CEO of Prosper, Inc., a leader in one-on-one coaching, with courses in entrepreneurship, e-commerce, internet marketing, real estate investing, personal finance, and stock market investing.

Ethan has made a significant contribution to the distance education industry by training more than 40,000 entrepreneurs in 73 countries. He was named a 2005 Ernst and Young Entrepreneur of the Year and a 2006 NRCC Business Man of the Year.

Ethan has owned and operated more than a dozen businesses, including Education Success Inc, Money Mentor Center, Prosper Media, and AdCafe.

Services Available

Ken Blanchard and Don Hutson speak to conventions and organizations throughout the world. They also have content available in audio CD and DVD formats, as well as Internet-based training.

The Ken Blanchard Companies conduct seminars and in-depth consulting in the areas of customer service, leadership, team building, performance management, and quality. Don's firm, U.S. Learning, specializes in sales growth, relationship enhancement, management, and entrepreneurship.

For further information on Dr. Ken Blanchard's activities and programs contact:

The Ken Blanchard Companies
125 State Place
Escondido, CA 92029
www.kenblanchard.com
1.800.728.6000 from the United States
1.760.489.5005 from anywhere

To find out more about **Don Hutson** addressing your meeting or working with your company, please contact:

Don Hutson, CPAE, CEO
U.S. Learning, Inc.
516 Tennessee Street, 2nd Floor
Memphis, TN 38103
901.767.0000 (phone)   901.767.5959 (fax)
Don@DonHutson.com
www.DonHutson.com

About Prosper:

Prosper, Inc. is a recognized global leader in distance education for entrepreneurs. Founded in 1999, Prosper has helped over 40,000 students discover and then leverage their entrepreneurial strengths to build successful businesses.

Prosper believes your education should pay. Their one-on-one coaching methods deliver accelerated results in the following areas:

- Entrepreneurship
- Small Business
- eCommerce and Internet Marketing
- Real Estate Investing
- Online Stock Market Investing
- Personal Finance

To learn more about Prosper's one-on-one coaching, call 1-866-704-4028, or visit their website at **www.prospering.com**.